For Etsuko -
For guiding me into
Nichiren Buddhism during
my last decade.
I must have done something
terribly right in my last
life to deserve this.
With love,
Joanna
July 2014

CATCHING LIGHT

collected poems of Joanna McClure

Foreword by MICHAEL MCCLURE

Edited and with an introduction by
CHRISTOPHER WAGSTAFF

North Atlantic Books
Berkeley, California

Published by
North Atlantic Books
P.O. Box 12327
Berkeley, California 94712

Frontispiece photo by Wallace Berman
Cover and book design by Jasmine Hromjak
Printed in the United States of America

Catching Light: Collected Poems of Joanna McClure is sponsored by the Society for the Study of Native Arts and Sciences, a nonprofit educational corporation whose goals are to develop an educational and cross-cultural perspective linking various scientific, social, and artistic fields; to nurture a holistic view of arts, sciences, humanities, and healing; and to publish and distribute literature on the relationship of mind, body, and nature.

North Atlantic Books' publications are available through most bookstores. For further information, visit our website at www.northatlanticbooks.com or call 800-733-3000.

Library of Congress Cataloging-in-Publication Data
McClure, Joanna.
  [Poems]
  Catching light : collected poems of Joanna McClure / foreword by Michael McClure ; edited and with an introduction by Christopher Wagstaff.
      pages cm
  Summary: "This collection of poems will appeal to poetry lovers, feminists, and Beat culture historians interested in discovering—or rediscovering—the works of an influential yet seldom publicized 20th-century American poet"—Provided by publisher.
  ISBN 978-1-58394-613-8
  I. Wagstaff, Christopher, 1943– editor of compilation. II. Title.
  PS3563.C342 2013
  811'.54—dc23

2012045592

1 2 3 4 5 6 7 8 9 SHERIDAN 18 17 16 15 14 13

For my daughter, Jane—
You are forever amazing, an unexpected delight in my life,
and a gift to the world.

Contents

IV. WHISPERED UNIVERSE WHORLS (1970s)

VIII. TIME LOOSENS HIS GRIP (1980s)

IX. THE COREOPSIS ARE BRIGHT AGAIN (1980s)

X. Our Love Overleapt the Chasms (1990s)

XI. LIKE AMOEBAS WE COOPERATE (2000s)

Acknowledgments

I would like to thank Richard Grossinger and Lindy Hough for their lifelong commitment to cutting-edge poetry and literature, starting with their founding of the literary magazine *Io* in 1964. Their original vision continues to be kept alive by the dedicated staff at North Atlantic Books. My thanks to Jasmine Hromjak for her design work, to Kat Engh for her promotion work, and to Adrienne Armstrong for all her copyediting. My special thanks go to project editor Jessica Moll for her gentle but firm guidance in keeping me on track and helping me work through various decisions along the way.

My thanks also go to Brenda Knight, who first noticed there was a gap in information about women of the 1950s, and who then set about researching, writing, and getting published *Women of the Beat Generation*. The poetry readings she organized (we called it "going on the road") in the San Francisco Bay Area with the four remaining women writers here were a delight to be part of—each of us so entirely different, so entirely who we were then.

I owe a great deal to Michael McClure. It was a specific poem of his that drew me to him and to the wide range of the exciting art, music, science, and poetry world he inhabited. His instinct for the newest and most exciting people in these fields enriched my life no end. I am also indebted to him for urging me to select the poems in *Wolf Eyes,* which he published.

Wesley Tanner's friendship and art with Arif, his letterpress, were another gift. When I was choosing a cover for *Wolf Eyes,* he let me pick a color to match the eyes of Jethro—the wolf that had inspired that poem. When he decided to publish *Extended Love Poem,* he gave me the choice of a thousand ordinary books or a hundred fine print books on the finest paper with individual covers. I have never regretted the choice of the finer than fine book he produced.

Glenn Todd, writer, retired editor, and dear friend, thought there must be another book in the poems I had written over my lifetime. He took my large accumulation of poetry and began putting it all on his computer. Each week we would proofread what he had done and he would have me date them as best I could, and name those without titles. He also then edited the chapbook *Catching Light,* from which this book takes its title. When finished we celebrated with a large collection of nine hundred poems divided according to decades.

The final piece came when Christopher Wagstaff took that accumulation of poetry and began studying and working with it to extract the book that you now hold. With his genius for sorting and arranging and his fine and discerning intellect, Christopher was able to select poems from many genres and weave them together into a book that flows effortlessly.

I also want to thank Lawrence Jordan for these last twenty-five years in which our lives have been intertwined. His home and garden have been a refuge of delight for me. His constant care is a mainstay in my life. His respect for my poetry and his love and support for me are deeply appreciated.

The life teachers to whom I am forever indebted live on in me though they have since died. They are Edith Markson, founder of American Conservatory Theater; Frances Miller, parent education administrator; Cheryl Shohan, Center for Attitudinal Healing; and Fariborz Amini, psychoanalyst and early childhood consultant.

Hully Fetico, bodyworker and guru, still here, remains an inspiration—a living example of spirit and courage—a true life force.

Thich Nhat Hanh and his writing have been a major influence on my development starting in the 1990s. Other key writings have been those of Stephen Levine and Lama Surya Das. Even earlier, I owe thanks to M. Esther Harding for her book *The Way of All Women,* in which I was able to see myself in her chapter on "The Ghostly Lover" and make a change in my life's course.

My mother and father, in their love for one another and for my brother and me, leave a legacy of courage, independence, and spirit. Allowing me to give them my money to gamble with in bridge games (which they usually won) probably gave me my real love of gambling with life. My brother's lifelong support, his intelligence, his romantic dreams and adventurous life continue to fill my heart—our bond is a true treasure. I also send blessing to my grandfather Kinnison, who visited each year from Texas with a large bag of pecans and walked on his hands for the amusement of us children—teaching me that age should not dampen spirit.

FOREWORD

In the swirl of her life, the friends and stars in Joanna McClure's constellation included Robert Duncan and Jess Collins who presented the idea of a household of art and life. Wallace and Shirley Berman gave her the gift of an open style of living. Jay DeFeo presented alchemy and endless depth, and Robert Creeley brought quicksilver energy and wit. Not far below Joanna on the slopes of the Downey Street Hill in the Haight-Ashbury the whole counterculture lifestyle was being pulled together. Her hilltop windows looked out on the waves crashing against the cliffs of Point Bonita in Marin County. The parade of wild-eyed and soft-eyed young geniuses of music, glass art, oil paint, and collage swirled through San Francisco to the Be-In and on to Big Sur or Mexico. Katherine Jane, a beautiful blonde daughter named after a child of Kenneth Rexroth's, was born. All this in the midst of one of the richest substrates to be imagined—and it was all in its early days. People were beginning to relate to living on the Pacific Rim facing Asia. A romantic poetry was being born with old cars trudging to the top of Mount Tamalpais, and in the elegance of thrift shops, plus I. Magnin department store, and fairy tales by George MacDonald. Conversations were as good as Drambuie by the fireplace; instant coffee and the discovery of health food were a part of it all. The poems in *Catching Light* have no ambition, exactly as yellow violets and golden tracks-of-spring growing on the nearby Twin Peaks have no ambition. They arrive uniquely, sui generis, each one an entity, coming out of the substrate into the fog and sun. Once Diane di Prima stayed a while at the large farmhouse-like flat. A few times Charles Olson's big boots left scuffs on the wooden floors. This world had become just right for shaping the *yugen*-consciousness of haiku into the emotional shapes of Joanna McClure's energy-oriented imagistic poems. It was all new. Sight, sound, taste, touch, smell were the qualia along with the Arizona sound from her childhood. To experiment and to discover, she bent her head by lamplight to translate Gerard de Nerval or searched for the real Lorca hidden behind the meek translations of those days. Her poems stacked themselves in dark wooden drawers on scraps of writing paper and pages torn from pale blue notebooks. Was there a desire to flaunt or publish them? They are part of a deep passionate heart where beat meets black mountain by way of san francisco animism.

She may have said, "No, I have no desire to publish. It's interesting to read the new authors' writing that is appearing, but publication is not for me.... Maybe someday ..."

In 1974 I published *Wolf Eyes,* a selection of her poetry. Readers and friends who found the book loved the forthrightness, the clarity, and the music of the poems. Small publishers were coming into being and were busy lining up new literary movements, but it was a men's club, and gifted women who were the supports for their artist husbands and lovers were left with their art ignored.

Now *Catching Light,* Joanna McClure's collected poems, is here. No holds are barred in this writing; we can read Joanna McClure alongside Pound, Lenore Kandel, and D. H. Lawrence.

Michael McClure

INTRODUCTION

Among the many arresting voices of the Beat poets and writers of the San Francisco Renaissance, Joanna McClure's warm, naturally grounded, visionary lyricism sings out clear and reassuring as birdsong. Born to Almyr and Ramona Jane Kinnison in 1930, she spent her earliest years on a fifty-thousand-acre cattle ranch northeast of the Catalina Mountains in Arizona. After the ranch was sold in the middle of the Depression in 1935, the family moved to Tucson. During adolescence Joanna was especially devoted to her father, whose gentleness, generosity, humor, and love nourished her. His long bout with Parkinson's disease was painful for her, and she mourned not being able to alleviate his disabilities.

At a young age Joanna became aware of her intimate link to animals and the natural world of the desert and the nearby pine-forested mountains. In addition to chipmunks, a goose, a number of cats and dogs, two baby mountain lion cubs who were found on the ranch, and a goat she won in high school who lived on the front lawn, she had a beloved paint horse who boarded at a dairy and came to town once a year for her to ride in the rodeo parade. Her older brother shared Keats' and Shelley's poems and philosophic ideas with her. Walt Whitman's poetry helped her see how she could identify with the people and things around her, and his *Leaves of Grass* literally "saved my life during my terribly anxious fifteenth summer," she has said.[1]

Joanna attended the University of Arizona, where she studied the sciences and humanities and later met undergraduate student and budding poet Michael McClure, who moved her with his passionate, expansive vision and introduced her to the music of Bartok, the novels of James Stephens, and the poetry of Yeats and Pound. The connection between the two was profound, and a year or two later they became a couple in San Francisco. In 1956 their daughter, Jane, was born, an experience McClure said shook her whole being.[2]

Michael and Joanna became part of the burgeoning poetry and painting renaissance in San Francisco (as they later would be associated with the hippie scene in the Haight-Ashbury), which revered the imagination and sought its infusion into life as well as into art. The couple came to know a number of artists and poets who were crucial to this artistic flowering, an influence on Joanna being the poet Robert Duncan and his partner the painter-collagist Jess, whose devotion to literature and creativity as life commitments rather than avocations spoke to her. On one occasion when the McClures were ill and in need of help, Duncan and Jess took them into their De Haro Street apartment, caring for them and their six-month-old baby for a week until they recovered.[3]

After the birth of her child, McClure began reading Erik Erikson and Bruno Bettelheim and studying developmental psychology, and the desire to make things work between parents and children became a passion. In the early 1960s she became director of the Sunset Cooperative Preschool, where for the next thirty years she was continually involved in the exciting discoveries of early childhood brain development. Robert Duncan has noted that despite Joanna's invaluable involvement with small children and their parents, it was clear by the mid-1970s that she was not "just the wife of Michael McClure" but someone with "a very distinctive body of poetry" that people wanted to read.[4]

In 1957 McClure wrote one of her first poems, in which she clarified for her and Michael some of her basic beliefs, which included

"Desire for freedom, bodily beauty, tenderness, / And your love and your desire for change and Truth." Over the next fifty years flowed a steady stream of more than nine hundred poems, most of them written on scraps of paper, on yellow lined sheets, or in notebooks of various shapes and sizes. Often she would jot down her poems alone at night in her room after work, occasionally publishing them in little magazines when editors asked for a contribution.

The majority of the poems in this volume have not been in print before. McClure didn't promote her poetry or urge it on others, and *Catching Light* captures the exhilaration that can occur with the subordination of one's ego and desire for place and recognition. Michael's encouragement was instrumental in bringing about the publication of her first chapbook, *Wolf Eyes*, in 1974: "Michael had felt I had poems that should be printed. I think he even hoped in those early days that I might become a popular poet. He had me sort through my poetry during one vacation, and I recall making my own system of labeling them, one through five, with number one being my favorites but liking most all of them."[5]

. . .

In a recent interview Joanna McClure has commented that she's never quite sure what her poetry is or should be, and that it doesn't seem to fit into any category she knows.[6] She defines her poetry as "a timeless spirit exploring itself," and one encounters this spirit in her work, whether she writes of her own life or that of nature or the world. In her poems—notable for their directness, naturalness, and amazing conciseness—she seems to be speaking to herself and her readers from the core of her being, as well as from the standpoint of someone like others, sharing their emotions. Joanna's longtime companion, filmmaker Lawrence Jordan, has remarked that this volume "reads like a novel," telling of her daily adventures, joys, angers, loneliness, and sorrows, and tracing the evolution of a woman whose awareness appears to widen over the years until it is clear that underneath life's discords and fragmentation lies "a deep underlying harmony"[7] and that "like amoebas" we all cooperate.

Robert Duncan introduced McClure to the work of the modernist novelist Dorothy Richardson, who, like her contemporary, Virginia Woolf, proposed that intimacy bringing one right up to things and people is an immediate path to understanding. McClure would concur with Woolf's declaration in *To the Lighthouse* that it is "unity that [one] desired, not inscriptions on tablets, nothing that could be written in any language known to men, but intimacy itself, which is knowledge. . . ." McClure feels that a woman's mind differs from a man's in that it is often more concerned with connections than with moving in a straight line. "Women's poetry can reflect more of an internal world and is perhaps more exploratory," she has said.[8] Some of her poems point to the courage it takes to be a nurturer in a culture that prizes competition and external success.

After her thirty-three-year marriage to Michael McClure ended, Joanna discovered that "Living alone / There is no one / Here to blame" and that she had had more than her share of personal delight. Although being on her own was challenging, she declares, "What I seek now / Is my imagination, / My dreams, / My other world" and to be intimate with "new green growing knowledge." Facing rigidities in herself blocking such new awareness, she earlier says in a long, playful poem, "For it's hurdles / We're for / And hurdles / We needs."

Throughout *Catching Light,* along with friendships, love, sexuality, appreciations, her husband Michael, and many other subjects, McClure considers the process of aging, sometimes realizing that just being alive at any stage of life is cause for celebration. In one poem she says that age is teaching her not to use laughter to laugh at others and to let the need to constantly "do" drop away. She feels gratitude for the resilient—and often irreverent—self in her that can't be wholly crushed out by time. Referring to her own slow growth, she comments, "A slight edge / On fear, after fifteen / Years of struggle."

A significant phase of the absorbing life story these poems recount is the poet's recurrent desire for "immersion," submergence in the strangenesses and startling beauties of the everyday. Although McClure's work is personal and her voice distinctly, solidly present, the force of her individuality can diminish as she melds into what she sees, hears, and encounters, which, in the words of "To Wander Mad," makes her "tear at the roots / Of all this being called *me*." This finishing with reason, this "drop into imagination," which she likens to a "plunge into cold Pacific waves," results in stunning glimpses of sparrow hawks, sea lions, newts, gooseberries, hedgehogs, skunk weed, a whale, night herons, a fairy shrimp, spiders, ferrets, a wolfhound, and marigolds. In "Connections," she declares, "My reality / Lies in the voice / of the red-tail hawk. / My reality / Lies in the bent grass / where the deer lay."

Some of McClure's most profound and accomplished poems were written in the last twenty or so years. They include the surprising summation of her life called—tellingly—"Gratitude"; the mention of being suspended above the incessant call of duty in "Sometimes"—allowing "endless non-time to open the heart"; and the description of the writing she yearns to do in "I Want a Poem"—"I want a poem / As fine as / Musk ox fur." Increasingly concerned about the fate of endangered species and the deteriorating environment, she takes hard looks at the "Shame of these times / Created by my / Country—this / 'Advanced' technology— / With its lack of soul / Its lack of / Compassion as / It races toward / More goods / More prosperity / Less understanding / Less connection / Less heart." And in "Lust," near the end of this volume, she requests that her body finally be given to the fish in the sea or placed on an altar of sticks for the birds of prey to feed on; and, closing, says, "I long, long to join myself / Back, back into all that life / From which I came." These poems fulfill that longing.

Christopher Wagstaff

NOTES

I'm grateful to Barbara O'Brien for sharing her editorial wisdom with me, to Rosa Monterroso for helping to format and keyboard the entire text, and to Jessica Moll at North Atlantic Books for our pleasant year and a half of preparing this book. And thank you most of all to Joanna McClure for the delight of working together.

1. Joanna McClure, unpublished interview with the editor, December 8, 2012. Many of the details in this short sketch are from this discussion.

2. Joanna McClure, "Imagination and Writing, Part II," an unpublished and undated statement.

3. Joanna McClure, "Imagination and Writing, Part II." In this short essay Joanna touches on some of the challenges faced in the later 1950s:

There were raging fights, there was infidelity, there was a search for new visions in drugs, there was my depression and the anchor of a very strong lively child. And at its lowest ebb, at the new large flat on Fillmore [Street, in San Francisco], bare with only wires from the center of the ceiling where lights had been and in need of paint and without a stove even, Jess came to turn the wires into lights, Rexroth helped carry up a beautiful cast iron wood/gas stove, Larry Jordan helped Michael paint the walls, and I carried up and down the three flights our "things." The miscarriage that followed was followed in turn by bad flu, so that the family was hanging by a thread. It was then that Robert and Jess literally took us in.

4. Robert Duncan, unpublished interview with Eloyde Tovey (Berkeley: University of California, The Bancroft Library, 1978), 96. Duncan mentions Joanna McClure as one of the "loners" whose work doesn't "fit in with the story of [poetic] developments," but nonetheless has an important place.

5. Joanna McClure, "Imagination and Writing, Part I," an unpublished and undated statement.

6. Joanna McClure, interview, December 8, 2012.

7. Alfred North Whitehead, quoted in Chang Chung-yuan, *Tao: A New Way of Thinking: A Translation of the Tao Tê Ching* (New York: Harper & Row, Perennial Library, 1975), from the back cover.

8. Joanna McClure, interview, December 8, 2012.

I

LISTEN TO THE HOLY CROWS
(1950s)

POETRY

Listen, listen, listen
One out of five will glisten—
Dazzle your mind,
Create a bind,
Catch your senses,
White out your attention.

1957

Dear Lover,

Here on the eve of everything and humility,
The new shoes—the new tooth—
Can't quite fill the gap left
By Khrushchev, the rally, the gas chamber,
The satellite beaming down from the moon.

Your nerves ajar,
Mine apart.
Ghostliness, the promise of a
Dark change, hovers
Without motion
Between us—

Blocking the beautiful love felt two nights ago
And renewed by this pressure—
The pleasure of its discovery still fresh
Again last night.

Where are we?
Why the pain—so sane
And yet without purpose,
our plight?

You say you are an American—of the continent—
But it doesn't help your twitching nerves
Or the discouragement of being here, now, at this time
Sat upon by the pressure of these lunatic affronts.

I come from dusty desert mountains
Where people only killed other people, bad people,
And rattlesnakes and deer to eat
And valued their horse and families.

I have only lately learned to wear pointed shoes with delicate
    straps
And realized the value of a pearl choker with
High delicate necklines and short black gloves
Topped by wild cropped blond hair.
And I am glad and would wear them through a war
If I had to.

But these are not the battles I choose
These are only discoveries, like last night's love,
Which I want to fill a lifetime with
In order to stand a symbol of the things I still believe in . . .
Desire for freedom, bodily beauty, tenderness,
    and your love and your desire for change and Truth.
There isn't anyone on our side, just here where we stand.

And it's been too long
To make it all right again.

I can't defend them anymore
Or, more painful, cannot disengage
    From this time or place and have no desire
For any other time or place but my own.
A stubborn determination born somewhere in the struggle.

I've turned down too many gods to
Start inventing my own now
Or believe in yours either.

I only sit and wait and care for you
And worry—for I wanted to spend my life
Fighting with you . . . but
I wonder—what happens to us
When everything breaks apart.

My femininity is not willing to carry me along through sudden
    change.
I wanted to die slowly of old age.
The sliced lily plant, still green, hurts me.
I have no heart for wars I can't fight
Or bombs that destroy.

HOLY CROW

The lovely girl
    in the black turtleneck
pulls alongside the Captain's Buick roadster (picks her nose)
and watches amused through his eyes
until they are passed.

Thus I refute thee—Sapir.
        (people in caves watching shadows—Plato)
I am without language
Yet I feel, think, and know
        Without symbols
No reflections, confusions, conventions—
I refuse them all!
        and yet
I live exist and have within me

        bone thoughts as valid and hotter
        than many a poet's dead limbs
                Bah!

Conventions of all sorts bind us. The error is
not in the conventions but in the inability
to listen to the Holy Ghosts (Holy Crows—Holy
Cows).

The Holy Crow of my existence
    flaps to and fro—cawing
    confusing beating me with his feathers.
Help—help, you blind and fuzz my eyes so
I shall never find my way—
        Holy Crow—leave no dead wood.
        I cannot, no cannot, endure this blur of enlightenment.

POEMS FROM A WIFE

Poems from a
   wife who drank too much
     coffee—
to a husband I really love, love, love

     dein
      Blümchen

HYMN TO AN IMAGINARY HUSBAND

(Who Went to Sleep)

I love to cover you
Or uncover you
Or discover you
Or put you away on the shelf
For awhile

I love to lie with you
I love to play with you
I love to lie by you
I love to be with you
And I like to go away

I think I see you
I glance at you or
Around you
I look over you
I overlook you

I search for you
     Or
I find you
Keep you, hold you,
Feel you, look at you
And adore you
With all my heart

The Black Point

He who has faced the sun steadily
believes he sees, before his eyes flying obstinately
all about him, in the air, a livid spot.

Even so, all young still and even more audacious,
I dared fix my eyes one instant toward glory:
a black point is settled in my avid eye.

Since then mixed with everything like a sign of gloom,
throughout, on each spot which stops my eyes,
I see it poised also, the black spot!

What, always! Between me and happiness forever?
Oh! No one but the she-eagle—bad hour for us! bad hour!
Beholds the Sun and Glory with impunity.

[Translation from Gérard de Nerval]

WEATHER

Last day of June

What shall I do with
Last year's thistles?

The summer began,
I typed again.

The sun is hot . . .
On my head . . . on the sand.

Bugs begin to gather
On my bright yellow suit.

Swatting, I deny
Flower kinship.

A caterpillar ate a
W h o l e pearly everlasting.

II

THE LORE CALLED "ME"
(1960s)

GOING

Oh, my love, oh, my love,
Don't despair.
Three more months and we'll be there

Three more months
And just a day
Surely isn't
Far away

And when we get there
And when we get there
We'll romp and play
And skip a day

And start revolving
Churning
Groaning
And off and away

To start
Three more months
And just a day.

I SAW THE DOLPHINS

I saw the dolphins and huge
turtles with wavy
mouths for the first time.

A dolphin swam over to look at
ME. I watched their human
motions with their strange
non-arms. The turtle's timeless
slow perception and horny-headed
monstrous strong crawl took me back
centuries and into yet another dimension.

EVENING POEM
*for Richard Brautigan
and Mike*

I love to listen
To men
Struggling hard
With words
And the power
Of ideas

I move among them
Calm
Thoughtful
And pleased

My own intelligence
Part
Of the atmosphere
But quiet

ENDLESS

May of this year began
the revelation of the circle
    The endless line
    The endless motion
    The perfected beauty

NEW GIFT

I began to love today.
I saw it in Mike's smile—
    around the chin
    the lines the smile made
    the teasing loving male
    scratchy beard, curled eyelashes,
    smile line slashed on the cheek.
No words to describe this new
    (and yet so very very long ago)
    love—a homecoming—
        release—
        exquisite pleasure—
        complete captivation—
        girlish flutter—
        absolute laughing adoration
    the necessity and joy of kissing and pressing
    something so terribly dear
    the joy of just being allowed to love
                again.
I am so grateful for this new gift.

Loss

There are not
Enough

Curving
Dusty roads

Left to hurl
Myself against!

    The loss
      The loss!

    . . .

Drunkenness
  is Zen also

And cicadas

    . . .

    The stars
    So bright
      (blaring out in the
       space between the leaves)

    . . .

    The road
    Momentarily lost.

SPRING

The young auburn woman, tender and delicate,
Aroused by so much innocence,
Said these words, very low,
To the young blond girl, in a gentle voice.

   "Sap that rises and flower that pushes open—
   Your infancy is a bower.
Let my fingers wander in the damp tangle
   Where the nipple of a rose glows!

   "Let me take drops of dew
   From the clear herb
Where the tender flower is bathed.

   "So that delight, my love,
   May light up your open face
As dawn the bashful blue."

   . . .

Her beloved rare body, harmonious,
Soft, white as an innocent rose,
White of true milk, and rose colored,
Like a lily beneath purple heavens.

Glorious thighs, erect breasts
Buttocks, loins, belly, a feast
For searching eyes and hands that seek
And for the tongue and lips and all the senses.

Little one, let's see—does your bed
Still have, beneath its red curtain,
The bewitched pillows that stir so often,
And the wild sheets? Oh, to your bed.

[Translation from Paul Verlaine]

NEVER AGAIN

I want to grow daisies and do
All my shopping at I. Magnin's

I want Mike to be rich
And me to be a movie star

I want to be autonomous
And love people and things

But never fall in love again

THE SURGE

The plants in the kitchen window
Are my biggest joy
And astonishment.

They are wild with life
And I revel with them

Each time
    my eye
        follows
            their surge.

Porsche Trip

The sparrow is after all a mockingbird—
The ride, a "trip."

I lost my nerve
At seventy on the freeway.

My stomach never caught up with the Porsche.
My heart got lost on the boardwalk.
    The sea reached out for my soul.

Verlaine captured my imagination.
Bonnard's "Lesbos," my sensitivity.

An old actor stood up suddenly to
Perform Lea—mad—surprised my admiration.

I stroke the Scottish mohair
And watch the tamed sensual curve it follows.

Flames lick the feet of Jean Harlow.

JUNE

Gypsophilas
Purple velvet blouse

Sweet Williams
Rat crouching in a forest of sheepskin.

Schubert resounds monumentally
Pink salmon sits on dinner plates.

What shall I do
When the Nerval translations are finished?

OUT

I have thrown everyone out OUT
Put them to bed
Hung up on them
Lost my notebook

And a secret happy smile
Steals over me in the hallway
As I pad into bed.

A Separate Life

Time lives
A separate life.

It continues.
I come . . . and go.

Neither of us
Records the other.

Lesbos

I began to find women attractive at twenty-eight
At thirty-three I kissed one
At thirty-five my gestures seem awkward
    and rough with awkwardness.

Men are simpler.
Sex seems less differentiated.
Passion less tolerable.

Liz's breast and flashing smile.
Shirley's head, neck, and hips.
Patti's curled mouth and taste.

Felicia, blackgirl, you caught my heart on sight.
Timotha, I dared kiss you, because I cared,
And the night was wild.

Joan, your words "Doo Boon" drew out of me
      a sudden strange new passion
that stretched out—taut—across the long,
      long table,
Making others disappear.

THE FEAST

There was your presence, your words "Doo Boon."
An instant answering strange new passion rose within me.
I sent my soul back across the long, long table.
Taut, it made others disappear, as it stretched toward you.
"Boon Doo" I echoed. My heart thumped time
Deep inside my stomach as this mystery,
Still unsolved, uncoiled before me.

GONE

Can I fill out the forms
When life is empty?

I will remember what to do
But they will wonder where I went.

In time, a year or two,
When hope is dead, long dead

Will life appear
Once more?

DEATH

Today, Mother called
Today, Mike's play
Today, the shock of his death
Today, the misery of his death
Today, the irritation from his death.
    Tonight, the aloneness
This afternoon: the numbness
The "high" feeling in the legs
       the small of the back
the desire for a touch.
Tonight: my tired face, transformed,
   temporarily joins the
   success of the play—the excitement:
Afterwards a slow sudden return
   to despair, to tiredness
A faint search for what comfort?
A feeling of rightness at being alone.
A sadness at being so alone.
    Mike plays the autoharp
    Jane sleeps at Louise's
    I am lost, afraid, and sad.

MONKS

I love monks with shaven heads and huge eyes
And the way they move at Tassajara.
I love watching our wolfhound lay out and run
I like the feel of long hair, mine,
The look of short hair, Mike's

The house is full, full, full
And beautiful
He struggles monumentally
Writes hard, ecstatic
Visionary poems

I sew
The floors are kept clean
And we do not consider money.
We may be
Misplacing it.

The wind howls
The cold outside is biting
There are new spreads on the beds
Our Christmas tree has a new
Chinese twist at the top.

ON BEING A WOMAN

At thirty-seven
I discover
The basic sexual
Powerless part of being a woman.

The soft calm
And acceptance of the difference
Brings a new dimension
Of beauty.

Truth creeps so slowly into my life
The satisfaction it brings spreads out
                    infinitely
The pleasure and expectancy of other truths
                    to come
Are a source of strength and warmth.

Each one settles my totality more firmly
And Mike brings me hashish.

THE EYEHOLE

Writing is that
Edge—
Which waiting
Then
Demands.

Pulled through
An eyehole,
The point
Becomes turgid.

Time tenses.
Energy and focus
Produce the
Bright now
        Sentence, word—
                    Silver polished.

The Music Stopped

It feels like I'm twenty-eight and depressed
Except my bones ache
And the horn music outside
Doesn't make me happy.

It will pass
Music will come again
I will feel again
But now

All music has stopped
A new stance is required
Must I suffer long
To discover it?

Life seems extra difficult
I strive
And do not see beauty.
I fight
   and do not find fondness.

The quiet,
The deadly quiet,
Is setting in.
There are so few faces
To look forward to.
The quiet
The battle for real—
Shorn of all delicacies,
Illusions, hopes, aspirations,
Pleasant reminiscences, love—
Is here.

Lines of Falsity

Where have my depressions gone?
Turned to passing angry days every one.

The lines of falsity
Are written on our faces.

On mine, the lines
Run from nose
To mouth.

Lines formed from years
Of smiling, squinting,
Being there for others!

I would change it—
Feel the lines with my fingers—
Let them drop—
Allow a long upper lip
To take over.

Waiting for a smile,
But not wanting it
At that price.

"Laughter"—Lorenz—
"Is a defense."
To sit with ourselves
Is difficult.

The pain is
Too great.

THE TOTALITY

Why?

If I am surrounded
With Beauty

Is my face
Ugly and tired?

If I did not believe
In a totality

I could not stand
Either myself
Or Michael

Or the way I treat children
At school some days

. . .

The skin becomes smooth with knowing, sureness.
The room becomes colored when one sees.

ANOTHER PLACE

The world falls away
At the edge of the sea

And another begins
At the dim edge of eternity.

SOUL FEASTING

A miracle recurs
In the midst of absolute reality.

Work, work, work, work, work

Yes—but never prepared
For the blessing

    Delights from children
    A love recovered
    A daughter blossoming
    The work gone—the blossom

      Astounding

    Gleaming floors fill me
    The music endlessly
       beating

    My floors . . .
    I love each dark crevice
    My room . . .
    I love each reflection
    Each creation
    Each leaf, mountain, ocean.

Keep Off My Tracks

I sorrow not
I borrow not

I abbreviate
I sensualize

I re-devise
How to economize

And I throw it away
Like a bale of hay

Toward yesterday.

Keep off my tracks
These tacks advise, but
I lose vigilance
Prefer entrance.

Election Night Poem

Warm, moonlit night
The voting lines move slowly.

My mother is seventy.
A friend is dead at thirty-two.

Last year, raccoons
Moved silently, unnoticed,

Through shadows
Among the voters.

MICHAEL JOINED ME

Michael joined me
Today. Today Michael
Joined me.

We looked at the ocean
Afterwards, as
We walked above the cliffs.

Ivy, nasturtium leaves, a
Formal lawn and flower beds.
Where had the wildness gone?

I looked in hidden grottos under old trees
Secretly searching for it,
As I walked
    Immeasurably filled,
                by his side.

SELF-EVIDENT

I have a book.
He has one, too.

I like my book.
He likes it, too.

We simper.
We sigh.
We look then
And die.

We whimper.
We whisper.

We threaten
And deplore.

We explicate
Determinate

Rage and
Explore.

We hold it
Self-evident
And forever deplore

The other's
Insistence

On knowing
Yet more.

"Churlish
Insignificant
Untrusting
Insincere."

We excuse
Our insistence

On the other's
Shortcomings.

And search for
New mysteries
    to further explore.

I Wish

I wish your fiery eyes and intellect would focus on me as prey for
    just one afternoon.
I wish you would regard me with solid admiration, smiling
    curiosity, and endless pleasure.
I wish you would listen to all my thoughts and treat them to your
    mind's embroidery.
I wish you wanted to make me pregnant, make me yours.
I wish you wanted to read me new poems and tell me what tender
    things you saw and felt just now.
I wish you'd put your head in my lap, tell me your pain, and sigh
    with relief as I stroked your head.

I wish you dreamed of places to take me and never wanted to go
anywhere alone.
I wish you liked my smell.
I wish I had a curve that turned you on.
I wish you wanted to handle my head as tenderly as you did when
I went down on you.
I wish you touched my shoulders lightly, liftingly every day.
I wish you were always well and feeling good.
I wish you surprised me with new white hardtop Triumph sports
cars.
I wish you took me to the Pyramids and had time for me too.
I wish you blushed and told me your secret fears and loves.
I wish you wrote novels to amuse me.
I wish you remembered a time, place, or a kiss in our past that
you loved.
I wish you talked, or daydreamed, about our future.
I wish you did portraits of me.
I wish you loved me.
      And wore pajamas.

THE WALK

At 5:30 there is no one.
City streets are damp
With fog drizzle.

No one and myself
Pad softly, exploring
All that newness.

New again each day
New today
Just for me.

DEADLY NIGHTSHADE

Fresh—a week later—
Your pointed leaves
And graceful green
Teardrop berries

Brighten my vision
I would have eaten you
From love—
Learned the hard way.

I still love tomatoes

Solanaceae of my heart.

OLD MAN (TO GUIDE ME) . . .

I need an old man to love
An old man to tell me stories
An old man whose eyes I can look into
An old man to guide me
An old man to stand beside me

An old man to be sad with
      to laugh with
An old man to honor me
            protect me
            tell me stories
            take me places
            buy me things
            adore me   share his past with me
            keep away my pain
            as I keep away his age
             keep me busy charming him
         as I watch my image play for him.

PRIME OF LIFE

I am the wind
I am the wet leaves
I am the late hour
I am the winter out of season
     and summer when fall comes.

. . .

Recesses of my mind
Find me
Bind me

Jasmine catches
My senses
Heavy the weight
Of wakefulness.

Spider

A spider here so late at night
Drops down like Colette herself
To keep the rhythm of the night
And accompany me with small delight.

Front protrusions investigate
Table, cheese, and light.
Eyes roll with heavy wariness
As striding about, a spider's presence manifests itself.

Sleep here my small bright pet
Do pass the night near my small light.
Keep spider brightness close nearby
And stay with me tomorrow yet.

Play

She: Fudge crunch.
  He: Nuts.
She: Fudge crunch.
  He: Nuts.
She: Fudge crunch caramelized with walnuts.
  He: Nuts, baloney, baloney.
She: He loves me.
  He: He hates fudge crunch.
She: He loves me.
  He: He abhors candy.
She: I'm sweet and delicate.
  He: She tyrannizes.

She: I melt in his mouth.
    He: She gags me.
She: Will you always think me dear and sweet?
    He: You'll endure forever.
She: I'm a mountain of sugar.
    He: Floating in an ocean of shit.
She: My aspirations pierce the clouds.
    He: She stumbles on her own shoelaces.
She: I see stars—but they are real living spirits.
    He: She's blind, deaf, and immovable.
She: Listen, they're playing soft music.
    He: Perhaps she'll be quiet now.

THE ALPHABET

Today I discovered the joy of
The Alphabet.

Each of thirty children
Accessible—through method.

The joy of discovery is
Ceaseless.

    Can I teach this? Or only the
    Pleasure of discovery?

DELETE

Cancel these
Vain pages.

Cancel my
Non-universe.

Cancel me
    For now!

VODKA

One shot of vodka
             Stands
Between   my mind and
                    me

Pants spin in the dryer
Refusing to dry

While I
Put out my mind

And don't find
Another place to be.

Endless Pain

When love is gone
Life stands still.

The pain stretches out endlessly.
Memories mix hurt and anger,

With a few twists
Of faintly remembered pleasure.

And all darkness
Becomes gray and meaningless.

The Process

Dance away
Suffering.

. . .

Laugh, disdain
Caring.

. . .

Grow to be
Growth.

. . .

One must
Lust.

. . .

I will push
Away

. . .

The pain.
Create afresh

Its new
Desire.

I will
    Revolve
        Revive
            Restore

                the lore called "me."

CARING

Sharing—it hurts.
Sorrow knots my chest
with anguish.

I glimpse   a sweetness
departing over the
horizon—

Enchanted with
its grace
and
truth—

While I hold
the knot
and . hardly . dare

Hand it to you
to untie—

The sharing . being .
itself . the knot.

SPARKS FLY UP

My soul jumps
To unite with that
Above.

The ache of
Constant misses
Fans the desire
 Anew.

I would meld
With all that
Remains beyond my
 Reach—
  or
 Learn to leave
And then return
And care and say
 Goodbye

And catch the tender torment
Here and now, and bounce it
To *my* tune—instead of being

Rubber-banded in and out—
Yo-yoed on a devil's string
Of desire and doubt, and yes and no.

MUSEUM

White, white, white—
Shine white cotton

Crisp white bleached cotton blouse.
The young girl did not know

Wally Berman was dead.
She did not know.

The gallery was white
And cold, then, suddenly

With his sudden death
(His motorcycle crashed again in front of me)
She, too young and shocked,

The place too cold and formal
Yes, a funeral parlor, but there

Was no priest. I mumbled
Apologetically "I'm sorry . . ."

It was a beginning and then
It was an end.

Crosses—Seminas—Eyes—Noses

Artists—I Loved and Didn't Love—

My admiration remains
    past stillbirth exploded
    past infidelities consummated
    past unforgivable photographs
    past blue and red paintings

past habit and love and hate and
curiosity and history
which put us all
here together now
bedfellows as we were then
exposed not to history
but still with our privacy
     barely surviving privacy
      into the new era
       without "what" to
        conceal, to study,
        to know,
         to be.

HATE NOTES ON DAVE'S AUERHAHN STATIONERY

I hate liberals
I hate wild-eyed revolutionaries
I hate litterateurs
I hate my husband
I hate rich people
I hate psychiatrists
I hate deadened people
I hate singing fraternity people
I hate small-town minds
I hate big-city aplomb
I hate pretention
I hate clubiness
I hate politics
I hate some children
I hate bigotry

I hate pettiness
I rage at crowds, dumbly clapping.

OUTLINE

It rains outside
And drips big puddle-splashing drops
The outline of the redwood tree
Is stolid, uplifting.
I am happy in the midst of hardship.

I like my brandy
My pearls
And the thirties are a relief.
I couldn't have survived many more years of twenties
Without looking sixty.

Michael, I don't love you.
You are part of my life.
I would be empty—lost without you,
And I will love you again

You are like the redwood
I watch outside
Big—uplifting—alive—growing.

When I loved you so much
I had no idea of how I would
Cherish and admire you now.

Your body grows more beautiful
Each year.

I am grateful to us both
Simultaneously.

The problem is one of staying alive
I glow and you shoot fire
I am proud
Of what we are

Of what we have created
And left alone
Between us.

A Letter to My Daughter, Who Will Be Four Years Old

Dear Jane (Katie)—
I like you in all your guises,
                    disguises
and costumes. I love your
                    wailing
    sitting, flailing, teasing.
I love your round tow-head
    and your round toes
I love your round cheeks and
    your round nose and your
    shiny eyes—red like a cat's,
Or round and big with the threat
    "If you don't I'll cry."

I like your teasing and playing
  chuckling with unrestrained glee
  at your newest trick.
I love you busy and excited on the street
  creating your own world
  using ours—"Hi Hi—(a nice man)"
  and off again.
Every day like a kaleidoscope
  turning it this way and that
  rearranging, delighted
  MAD—IT WON'T WORK—FIX IT.
Dancing—arched, self-consciously beautiful
                Movements
So vitally aware of each gesture
Standing also stopped directly aware
  of the applause, stopped for one
  moment in the pleasure of an
  audience—surveying it—your domain
          and on
To the next step, the next game, the
next room, the next boredom which
  creates the cry the demand:
        "I never have anyone to play with
        Who's going to play with me?
        You told me we would . . ."
And so pushing manipulating charming
  pouting or
        "I'll tell my grandmother if you don't!"
        Eyes opened wide with simulated rage—
        Testing
And how am I to ever write a poem
  about you?
For there's no end to you

And I have forgotten the beginning
which lay in a deep desire I felt
for your father who was going away for a few days
And really had nothing to do with you.
    Except maybe that
the desire was strong enough to set in
motion a little girl who will never stop
    growing, becoming a living Love,
        A living tribute to love, an offering to the world and Love!

ANACHRONISM

Spider plant
With all your babies
Hanging heavily from you
With cracked
Dry dirt and
Uncovered roots

You thrive
Reach out the window
And BLOOM!

III

A STEP INTO SPACE
(1970s)

PORTRAIT
for Jane

Two songs are not enough

Your gentle quick eyes
Look out at me.
Your full parted lips
And soft flowing hair

Are only the outward signs
Of all I value in you.

But they speak
And speak well
Of all you are.

The openness—
A sign of generosity,

The slight slant
At the edge of your left eye
Bespeaks your ready wit
Your quick humor—

The right eye is deeper.
Its trace of sadness
Bespeaks your depth
Your capacity to feel
To be hurt—to know.

Your nose—its freckles
Show your honesty
Your straightforwardness.

Soft neck—
    Your youth
    Your promise.

Child of light
    You came to us
    And I am grateful

[Written looking at a photograph of Jane]

MY KIND OF MAN

Oh, I've got a real lover
I find him from time to time.
He's my kind of man
From dirty toenail—to flashing mind.

I met him very young.
There's been a lot between.
And every time I find him
It's something new again

We fight together—fuck together—
Think together—go crazy in turns—
Return together—remain apart.
Start again . . . struggle against
Each other—the Universe—our desire.

And now, it seems
We begin life together.
What weirdnesses shall we create?
What beauties consummate?

My being shakes with fear
as I begin to *ca pi tu late.*

SLOT OF TIME

My work is done
I am home
I have one day alone

The wind blows
The bell knocks
My life calls.

A day of life alone
Is rebirth
A slot of time

A treasure
A secret
A me-ness

I hug it to me
A buckshee
An expanse of pleasure

The details . . .
 of no importance.

Women's Liberation Day—August 26, 1970

Today—Michael let me carry the groceries uphill
Three years ago—he began to carry things for me.

My personal liberation has been an uphill battle
Beginning with the babe tucked on my hip as I fled

My tyrant—raging for freedom, for equality.
How to fashion a position, with parts so different?

I have openings that must wait.
He has protrusions that have only to thrust.

I may, however, throw my high heel through a window.
Or curse him, witch-like, from a mountain of fury.

Today he types my poems, acknowledging a
Counterpoint to our lives, while I search out
                                    an end to an old poem.

Two weeks ago, drunk, he salutes
My rise from property to independence—
        acknowledges the uphill course.

Last Night

Tonight I sprang
Bouncing uphill.

Remembered your
Heavy hand—

As years ago
Hand on my shoulder

Pushing down
You gestured—containment.

I laugh
With pleasure

At the memory
Of our physical games

And look at
Newly treasured eyes

Set off by beard,
Age, lines of grace . . .

Wisdom, humor,
Dark innocent curling lashes.

I remember, too,
The feel of your strong arm

Encircling my waist
As I have so often wished it. Last night.

AFFAIR WITH AN OCEAN

The wind
Touched my
Waist.

I
Wished to
Respond.

But
Knew not
How.

. . .

Later—
leapt the
Waves

Strained
against the
Tide.

Escaped—
running from
An edge.

Stood—
planted
Leaning

           into it.

For Sterling, Naturalist-Mentor

Gooseberries look
   like sea urchins
   taste all right—then inedible.
   Sun will sweeten them.

The large blue unknown berry
   tastes medicinal.
   Am I poisoned?

Skunk weed does smell,
   of skunk.

The garter snake does leave
   an after-image. I
   stand transfixed by
   this sleight of hand,
   as he eludes me . . .
   a fourth time.

The pimpernel shines
   Orange, violet, and yellow . . .
   Its color disproportionate
   To its size.

Deer droppings, coyote droppings.
   How foxes sit in groups
   on logs, at trail crossings.

The hydra,
   busy waving mouth tentacles,
   you are all I see of a
   deep mysterious distant pond.

Vernal pond
>Your presence, absence,
>Ringed by green growth.
>In your center . . .
>Perfect, tiny
>blue flower
>yellow flower.

Out of Douglas fir—into chaparral
>A bare tall hill
>is the story of wind
>destroying trees.

Bushes collage together:
>Poison oak, coyote bush,
>Coffee berry, ocean sage (the smell) . . .
>Dark green, gray green, dark red poison oak, Bonnard.

Horsetail
>Eighty feet high
>In prehistoric time
>grows in bamboo sections by stream bed.

Huge eucalyptus
>aged and thick,
>supports water pipes across deep canyon,
>hangs on cliff-side.
>Chains cut deep
>into its heavy lower bark—a healed wound.

A pair of mated red-tails
>Hang motionless . . . on an updraft
Vultures gather around . . . rising hot air
>waiting for a ride . . . up.

My Refusal

Michael, you come to me
Friendly, late at night,

And I send you away
In my need to be alone

The gift of your friendly gesture
Stays with me

As does the gift of
My refusal.

On Beginning the Last Half of Life

Forty—A wave crests.
A surge peaks.
With pride and strength
I ride the crest,
Look back,
Bid all look up.

Forty-two—The approach is slow
Slow—the size of the task
Emerges. A new surge
Now tugs. New forces
Create themselves. Call out.
New dignities arise.
New pools of serenity.

It is all different here.
Like Sido,
Will my next passion
Be a flower? A mountain?

There is a new taste to food.
A yellow cat lies
Warmly, on my knees.
Lately, I allow visitors.

FOR JOAN

A poem
Begins

Somewhere
Far inside.

Clear—it travels
Out.

Its mystery
Amazes us.

STOLEN

Today I revisited
The ocean,

Remembered—
A winter night

Filled with fog
Alone, there,

On the beach.
A momentary fragment.

Skipping school.
No one, no clothes.

Cold waves
Welcome

My intimate
Presence, stolen

From the gathering
Waiting presences.

Responsibilities—
Frozen.

DAILY DANCE

Tatters, chances, dances:
    Life rolls by on waves
Bouncing us above, below
    On sand, on snow

Out of ocean's reach
Safe on the beach

Or lifting us up and
Setting us down

Sucking us under
Throwing us up

Using us—to change the beach?

    "I would prefer not to,"
        Oh Bartleby—I envy thee.

YOUNG DEATH

Issa's daughter,
Bright one-year-old,
    Died.

An old lady cried
Over tomato plants
    Frozen before maturity.

I mourn my daughter—
For lack of passage
    Ceremony.

And cry for any young
Thing cut off from
    Blossoming.

THE THIRD DAY

I hurl myself at waves.
It has become
An angry communication.

My body, an invitation
For the lowest order
Of non-meeting.

Even my two
Most prized possessions
Work against me . . . now.

POETRY CAME THEN

To work, to work, to work again
To face the cold, white, hard page
With cold sober calm eyes

Poetry came then, before,
From over-exuberance
From intoxication.

Will poems assemble
Themselves, now, again
From within this new self?

. . .

3:30 in the morning
I wait quietly to see.
It is too early to walk.

Roots

Heavy rain runs outside—inside
Warm kitchen noises and wood fire.
Grayness stretches . . . outwards, a long long way.

Outside the window
Avocado leaves blow, energetically, north then south.
French broom wetly leans with the wind.

The redwood stands there . . .
Drips and glistens.
Inside, my toes reach for roots.

Ah, Here

Self-righteousness is
Guilt's armor.

I see it now in others,
Silent with dismay.

Watching—a pain.
No way to explain.

My wisdom a cross
To bear, if I care.

Where is my reward . . .
     Ah, here . . . this year's new maple leaves!

On Being Left in North Beach—Once More

In cold hate I see your profile.
Separate clean hatred releases
Former pain.

First a kindly hand touched my arm.
Next a hard voice edited me out of your universe.

Having been but insecurely perched there sideways
At best, this turn of the screw, adding pain to pain,

Unhinges rage—there being nothing further to lose.

And having lost, am restored nearly whole, extra hard,

To some fine inner self for which you have no use.

ICELAND

Vast land, vast land
Makes me smile.

Wool and eiderdown
Black rock and green pool

Ocean and peak
Space and air

Black eiderducks with white
Face the shore in a row.

Ground breaks up
In swells and cracks . . .

Unnerved, I breathe
Sharp clean air,

Stare at land
Still churning,
    Becoming.

New York

The bags go in.
The bags go out.

I lie down.
The planes now shout.

The air I can taste
With the tip of my nose.

Iceland's behind.
San Francisco's ahead.

Why can't I . . .
Proceed, or go back in time?

Baja

Moonlight on warm
Salt water.

Coyote shit
On fifteen-foot rock pinnacles.

   Sting
And fear of death

   in that soft
   ecstatic moonlit night.

Warm waves
On dark rocky beach.

INDIA

Palms, pool, cattle—
Boys jangling in circles
Dancing around fires
On night bridges—
    Buckshee, buckshee, buckshee.

    . . .

An idle listless long fingernail
Scratches mindlessly, aimlessly
Sensually for lice under rags.
The smell of excrement and mud.
    Paper, tin, and cardboard shacks.

FOR ROBERT AND JESS

Green wet moss
    and
I enfold
An image
    of two men
Who lead
as they precede
    our lives

Spotlighting
      corners

Forerunners
      of knowledge
Growing to stately
      height
As they study
      abstain
            refrain
                  accumulate
Rage and age
      on into some
            eternity of
                  light—
                        of night.

After Wesley

A napoleon
      of equal excellence
Delights my palate
      as your
            perfect printing
                  delights my eye.
      Exquisite creations.

A napoleon
      is not a napoleon
            is not a napoleon
                  is not a napoleon

As books
    are not books
        are just not books
            are just books

Or are such   special
      objects!

POET

Fat, huffing,
Late for—the event.

Staccato, rough bursts
Of whispered hissed
Admonitions—

Lapsing into
Quiet limp lines
Of dull despair.

Panted laughs
Snuffled snorts
Punctuated with
Machine-gun rapidity
    some private argument

Hissed, lurched out
While being swallowed back.

Menacing, low leaks
Of thought forced out—

Tightly held in the mouth,
Not wishing to be parted.

The argument is
Internal—eternal.

WHITE PEACOCKS

Trail long tails,
Shriek at the sunset

Where gray-blue water
Washes quietly against

Green and yellow cliffs
And owls hoot down

Lanes that lead
To ocean's edge where

Copses harbor lizards,
Pot holes, weasel droppings,

Feathers, lichen, coon
Corpses and tremors of

Here and now . . . and
Long ago . . . as barking

Sea lions form eerie cries
From floating seaweed.

Benjamin

Benjamin, philosopher prince
Of our porch,
If you went now
The satisfaction
You brought
And shared
Would live
Long after.

I stare at your
Enclosed presence—
Paws tucked under,
Ears laid back,
Whiskers at ease,
Svelte sleekness,
Mature composure.

A life well spent,
Well shared,
Not with your kind
But with us.

A small pleasure
To have missed
In return for
Total adoration,
Near deification
        and
Constant participation
In our lives
During these
Rich years.

FOR MIKE AND BOB PETERS

Poetry pours
Into my ears,
Healing with
Beauty—

A tonic for
My bruised soul,
Freshening

As I listen.
Secret ecstatic
Stars

Shoot about corners
Of my shoulder blades,
As an image sparkles

Out, into me.
Where? Why?
And why not?

My gratitude—
An exact measure
Of this now pleasure.

For Michael

Patience, love, yet—
Once again.

My longing
Plagues our life

As my laughter
Brightens it.

I would bring only
Laughter and loyalty,

Yet I suffer,
And am unfaithful.

Forgive me—all my
Peculiar loves.

Forgive me this
Eternal recurring pain.

I feel your hand
Now—again.

This Afternoon

Open to the wind's
Gentle touch
Through my hair

Caught, terrified
Being alone
With myself.

Angry, vicious.
Slip-sliding around
People.

Holding my vicious
Tongue, as the hissing
Of my soul

Silently looks about,
Looks away . . . from all those
Waiting targets.

THE AIR STILL AGAIN

The air is still again
One more summer/fall
        Meld together

        Soft pink sunsets
        My mother will be eighty
        I have had more than my share

Of personal delight.

I walk out to the deck
   Where does the light
      beyond the trees
         near the ocean
           come from?

CONNECTIONS

Rhythms re-establish themselves.
Tears come and go.

When did we first get connected?
Why does it still matter so?

Children yes, husbands yes,
Stained glass yes, mothers yes,

Grandmothers, *sí, sí, sí!*
But still I feel the web

Of another weaver, for facts
Won't ever account for all of this!

SENSORY RECLAMATION
for Peter Berg

Discover darkness
Re-experience breathing.

"My feet say to me
Run, there is joy in swiftness.
The size of the word is
Its own flight from crabbedness."

Can you hear water flow?
Waves crash? Swim,
Feel cold water,
The pull of current.

Smell water, test the air,
    sniff pleasure in the wind.
Time is tasted through
    the changes in our food.
Time stretches to infinity
    through a mushroom.
We experience cousin fibers of genetic strength
    through the animals we know.

Feel the wind—free your mind on clouds.
Catch a microcosm in a wildflower,
Allow your fingers to spin, weave, caress.
Startle with the birds.
Let water float you.

Build for the pleasure of the power of
        "being the cause of."
Sing: breathe and create.

VENOM

And so
What changes then?

The hour is
Four o'clock.

My insomnia
Has the twitch

Of venom.

Still.

This Evening

White balloons
Skyrocket into eternity

White peonies
Explode into my today

Children suddenly
Gone from my school

A father suddenly
Begins death

I am still here . . .
A buoy on the ocean,

An unsure touchstone—
Bedrock better than sand

In earthquakes, but
Liable to ballooning off

Over the ocean
If I live to be fifty
          and still care.

MOUNT TAMALPAIS

The full moon comes and goes.
Laurel tree guards over me.
Yet the tears knock:
"We're here again. We're here"

And I struggle—sad hostess—
Reluctant to allow remorse
Inside again

Impatient at never
Finishing.

PATTI

You hang out with
Persian rugs

New business
And sex,

Complaining as you
Tax yourself

To fulfill new
Roles, make

Money, and change
Your luck.

Viva the spirit
Of hope and . . .

Reincarnation which
You enact yearly

For us, your admiring
Audience.

IV
WHISPERED UNIVERSE WHORLS
(1970s)

WINETASTING

The haze of wine
        by candlelight
Brings new
        understanding.

Why not blur
        the edges,
Glow from within,
And taste sweet
        new fragrances?

ANCHOR

Oh, love, who loved me
Straight on
With the delicacy
Of a heart touched,

Whose shoulders
Shielded me,
Whose care
Tore me apart,

Brought springs of tears,
Emptying out of crevices
Long sealed and aching,
To soft new surfaces—

Slowness that soothed fear,
Honesty that protected,
Wryness that gave balance,
Choice of words that imprinted

Me beyond repair.
Tearing you/me out of my heart
Is a price I hadn't
Planned to pay.

And so here I say:
This pain, this day,
All your quiet disentwining
Finally spares me not at all.

The ache of loving you
Remains, a dark anchor,
Testimony to past delight
Now sinking back under.

THIS POETRY

Scents, es-sence, of me
Distilled, scattered—
A trace of something
I swallowed,

Then hallowed
With what words
I could find.

HAIKUS

Green fresh Christmas tree
Delicate hidden caverns.
   Me—decorate you?

. . .

Rain falls on our deck.
The school she-rabbit visits
   New wet turds join old.

. . .

Perfect dark pine tree
All covered with lights and balls
   I lost you somewhere.

CARNATION

for Lewis and Phoebe

Fragile, I sit with it,
Carnation, a question mark,
A gift from the evening.

My spirit failed
Outside the door filled
With busy voices.

Inside I leaned
On walls, on friends
On the hope of poetry

On the next generation
On any new discovery

On quick discreet kisses
On white walls
On the next champagne.

. . .

Other days
I am stronger.

RETURN

Return, return, return
Spin about
Try not to shout

While, meanwhile, inside
A TURMOIL of ecstasy
Questions, delights, breaks free

Feeling the air on my skin
  The space flying away
              beneath my wheels
    the touch of moonlight
              on my window.

Here I sit

Listening, detached, waiting
Excited by my shoulders

And this unexpected
                interior
                    reasonless
                        Pleasure.

SPACE TO MYSELF

A moment or so
To peruse my soul
A moment or so
To assemble the whole

A splintering night
A loss of free flight
This day descends
Like the fist of might

And I must prepare
To emerge intact
A small rubber entity
Reshaped by my breath

Rolling my best speed
Bouncing when high
Or lying deflated when
Stabbed by a love.

"Breathe me my life" I
Beg quietly then.

Space to myself—
A small kind of need—
Is viewed by him
As a sort of misdeed.

He eyes my privacies
With suspicion and greed
And gestures and grimaces
To end them full speed.

The higher my walls
The more he peers over
Jealous of secrets he
May never discover

Crannies of being
Where I might hide a crumb
Away from his grasp
Safe, alone, at last.

A golden crumb of me-ness
Existing as a tease
De-fining, fencing off,
Fi-nal ec-stasy of se-cur-ity.

. . .

Alone again at last
I grasp the space
To dance, delight

My inner light
   and
Savor safety
Here away from him
Who threatens me
The most.

NIGHTLIFE

for Downey Street, San Francisco

A raw egg thrown
Through clear starry night—

A clean
Near miss.

The excitement
Of neighborhood.

Parked cars
Blocking one another.

Loud horns.
Walk aways.

The continual
Drama!

Pinioned

I sit
Held there
Pinioned

By a
Vision
A voice.

Michael
Reads—twisting
My senses.

Heart, mind
Vibrate
To

Strange
   Complex
      Whispered
         Universe whorls.

Breathing falls back
The craft is
Overpowering.

Michel, Michel

Toujours gai
We make our way

To the banks of Paris
To the edge of the bay.

With a kick
And a sigh

And a blast
And a go

We argue
And stomp

And demand
Each new blow.

For it's hurdles
We're for

And hurdles
We needs,

And if they're
Not there

We'll make 'em
Ourselves.

For to screw
Ourselves up

And clear
The high pole

Is what
We like best.

To try
Each other

To settle
The test.

To run it
All out

To decide
What is best.

We'd invent a
New world

If it all
Went to rest.

For it's leapin'
And connivin'

That makes
For the fun.

And it don't
No matter

If we land
On our bum.

For it's
The skiddin'

And skatin'
That keeps us

In trim
And we's

Always thinkin'
Of ways to stay slim.

Wheelin' and
Wartin'

And making
A din,

It keeps
Us happy

It keeps
Us thin,

For when
We get fat

We can't
Abide that.

Morose and
Unmoved

We're sullen
And fat.

We lie
About—restin'

And wishin'
For action

And hopin'
We'll get thin

Just sittin'
And fastin',

But thin
We don't get

'Lessen there's
A bit of the action

And want it
We do

Though we hang
To the traction.

Toujours, toujours
Allons.

WHY SHOULDN'T I BE I THESE EIGHTEEN YEARS LATER?

I am not I
I was another I
I was a child I
I was a righteous I
I was a feverish I
I was a rebellious I
I was an ever-seeking I
I was an accusing I
I was an idealistic malcontent I
I was an incomplete I
I was a blind peevish I
I was a vicious unforgiving I
I was an occasional loving open I
I was a forever hopeful I
I was an unbelieving I
I was an unseeing I
I could not look, then.
I was embarrassed, then.
I was afraid, then.
I lingered and hoped, then.
I pursued the evasion of pain, then.
    I made the world in my image, then. It is all new now.
Formed, trapped, liberated, and bundled into
    All that I love.

Listening

Who—when—where?
Tear the event

From out the book.
Look again.

Discernment is here.
Bear the loss.

Celebrate the distinction,
Rely on vision,

Revisit the connection,
Refresh experience,

Resist replenishment.
Wholeness, I hear you.

Process

Our children
Are not

Our children—
Are part of

A process.

Now

Can you buy
My anger?

Can I switch
Off vengeance?

Would God let
Barter be . . .

To trade AWAY
My wrath.

This Year

This year is one of
Glamour and a honing
Of fine instincts

Mike and I react surely
Quickly. The pain
Remains, but the
Dealings are surer.

We create

     a

Wedge

To move the Universe

Our instruments

Are: Laughter
      Rage
      Beauty
      Ambition.

THE COASTLINE

To the South
It turns, winds, softens

The air warms
The smell thickens

As I breathe in a
New/old ecstasy

First carried—
Then searching

Pleased by the hunt
Tracing, as I pleasure

My feet, delighting in
    Touching coastline,
        Tracing a course,
            Hunting for that connection.

Toes reach out
Heart shines
The sun on the waves
Is soft.

ZEN FLOW

My body molds itself
Around warm smooth rock.
I should be ashamed
To let water hold me so . . .

Waist floating, turning, hips twisting.
Perfect freedom expanding . . .
Eyes break open on skies,
Boulders, cliffs, leaves, and half-hidden nests.

Voices, water rushing over rock, and silence
Mingle on delicate nerve ends—
Respond to these subtle vibrations
Which caress my thin ear-membrane.

        . . .

Later—eyes see night skies above—
As hot water and whitewashed walls
Enclose the present moment,
Frame the instant's experience.

I lie, looking up.
Deep black, bright stars look down.

WHITE SWEET PEAS

White sweet peas,
Strong and tall,
Growing from a thumb's worth of soil.

Your blossoms

Startle my eye, my mind.
Their persistence, like a white moth,

A continual surprise
To all my senses, a tribute to
Sudden beauty, and whiteness.

ON DECIDING TO BE MY OWN GUEST

I stopped at house after house.
The people I cared for were not home.

No one to admire me, my new beauty.
No one to offer a chill glass of white wine.

The presence of my family annoys me.
I wish to be my own guest.

BENJAMIN

Favorite Family Totem,
You love our fireplace.

For weeks you have lain
Beside the fire—on the hearth.

Today you burnt your nose
Exploring the not-yet-dead embers,

And still you are back
Nosing the ashes.

You sit ridiculously framed
Behind the fire screen.

Your sleek profile
Ignores the incongruity

It presents—as if rabbits
Belonged—behind fire screens,

Preening in front of all the world.

BUCKSHEE OF THE NIGHT

Three raccoons
    bandit up
the redwood tree
interrupt the silence

of these haikus—
noisy, clumsy burglars
out to steal a tumble
on an abandoned moonlit roof
scattering bark on the ground below.

2:00 A.M.

    Me
Alone at last again forever.
The unexpected spider crawls
Quickly to the ceiling—
    Hangs
        and
            drops.   Swings
                so gracefully
I catch my breath
As the leaf catches the late night
                acrobat.

"I Only Know That Poetry Is Necessary"
—Adele Stackpole

I miss my wolfhound.
Head flopped on front hound paws.
My child keeps his picture
        beside her bed.

Intense brown eyes, elegant recline.

What warm flesh comfort.
What possibility of
closeness without words.

Hound, your semi-human, semi-wild
Sensibility makes you a needed link,
a spirit talisman.

I would give my daughter
A horse, a dog, with which
to fill out her childhood.

And give myself the same,
To travel with further
into myself.

JANE HAS MY WARMTH

Jane has
My warmth
My vitality
My viciousness

She has
His wit
His egocentricity
Our looks

She brings
    Life
    Difficulties
    A surge.

His father dies
    dreaming of
    one last fling
    one last hurl at being.

THE RABBIT

The rabbit is mad
             to join us.
He sits on the window ledge
Leaps to the couch
Pulls at my pencil
Tears at my paper
Throws about the newspaper
Gnaws at the cushions
Submits to rough petting
Jumps, ears forward,
             into space.
Tunnels into the covers
Thumps across bare boards
Eyes wild—
     up for anything.

BABE

The lost squirrel monkey
Is eight inches long.
A perfect babe presence.
Astounding alacrity—animal greed.

Fierce agility. Your jerking eyes and
Frightened quickness frighten me,
Fascinate me
As I hold out each new grape.

BIRDS

Night herons hunch
  Wading the quiet pond
    A menacing stealthy pursuit—
      Heavy as they fly, land,
        Stolid as they perch.

We watch their drama
  From tall grass, trees—
    Against sunset,
      And freeway background.

A highlight for the contained presence
  Of pond
    Of heron
      Of egret
        Of calm ducks
          And occasional pelicans

The branches bend and sway
　Under the weight of night herons:
　　Hunched successful businessmen,
　　　　　　　　Executives.

The Journey

Lurching forward
　　Into time

The power of
　　　Holding back

Demands
　　The lurch

　　　. . .

A measured pace
　　　For others.

For me
　　　The struggle—uphill.

The downward
　　　Avalanche

As, dusting myself
　　Off—

A new beginning
      Pulls me

Slowly
      To my feet.
            Once more.

ALONE

Here again alone
Branches rustle
As they did then.

I sleep alone—
Turn restlessly
Unused to the pleasure.

The skies return.
Children join and
Leave my company.

Remembering weaves
Now with
My senses.

Silence
Is, as before,

Heavy with
Meaning—intimacy.

My space sits
Untouched

        Forty years later.

FRENCH FRUGALITY

Written on stationery
Interrupted by my name
I salute you

Nearing forty
Gathering our own wood
Folding paper bags

Wishing I lived
On brick streets
That were washed daily

   . . .

To think at twenty
I could fill a room
With chaos in twenty minutes

Leave eggshells
Strewn below me
Throw papers out the window.

   . . .

Those overblown times
Have helped destroy
My love of randomness.

. . .

I want to make soup
Carry a mesh shopping bag
Return all my bottles—each day.

Scrub my kitchen
Use perfect utensils
Grow fresh herbs

And make my own wine.

Us without You

Michael—twin spirit—
I review the past—
My strong commitment

(Never voiced, woven
Into our lives, proof
In spite of myself)

As I re search
Suddenly I re feel
Our stubborn passion knot.

As I trace the lines
That lead away,
Peruse a non-you universe,

My refusal threads
Its way to distant root tips . . .
As anguish

At the thought of us,
Without you, strengthens
All my ties.

BLOW UP / OUT

Male / female
   Female / male.

From birthing
   to
     Being birthed

Full of one—
   (another)
     Then being, becoming

The Other—my own
Full desecratory
   Satyr self.

Is This Not Poetry?

To shake
To sob

To plummet—
Are these not poetry?

The rat we must
Kill—

Is this not
Poetry?

Stepped on
Rabbit pellets?

The roof in
Moonlight?

Jazz at
3:00 p.m.?

An idea
At any hour?

    Death, suddenly,
    Wherever it occurs?

Tom

Tom, we didn't know you,
But we cared.
Jane sobbed, not knowing why,

At the hour of your death.
Your death was stubborn—
The doctors were impressed.

What strength or pain or wisdom
Lay behind your blank exterior?
What history or stories?

No matter.
You are closer now
Than ever.

Did you plan
This heritage or only
Plot your own success—or both?

No matter.
Now you lie in peace
And receive small honor and care.

A prayer,
A blessing,
Leaves for your death,

I send.

FOR RICHARD PRYOR ON SUNSET STRIP

The knife's edge
The razor's edge

The nervous giggle
The secret knowledge

The edges of consciousness
Where delight waits

The artist's cut
Into the forbidden.

THE RUN
for Peggi Oakley

The trees are damp.
My feet reach for
Heavy thick leaf covering.

My thoughts keep
Counterpoint
To time's energy spent—

To my breath,
Each new smell
My companion

Our constant exchange.

THE FLASH
for Ed Cross

You flash
A magnetism

Beyond the here
And now.

Did you get to look
There at the other side?

What lightning grace
Touched you?

From where that sudden
Flashing wit?

You draw us all
Around, electrifying

Us, illuminating the
Here and now

With rolling insights
You throw away

With the pleasure of
A dispassionate connoisseur

Sure of his gifts
And taste.

We gather . . . daily—
To ask about you,

Bring gifts, share
Compassion, and

Treasure the jewels you
Throw us with the grace

Of a king.
No wonder you have attracted

Such an attractive
        Entourage of
                Retainers.

IMAGES

Creeley yields
Images

As satisfying
As pulling

Out potatoes.

Your Space

for Joan MacIntyre

Thank you, Joan,
  For your invitation
   (a crack of light in a gray day)

   For your new home
    (its space suits me)

    For your touch
     (in everything around you)

      For your beads
        (to protect me—I feel the fluttering
          of blue leather wings treasuring me)

        For the gift of your mind
         (and sympathy so quiet tonight)

         For Ian
           (whom I could so instantly love,
            cherish, adore, and relate to)

           For your poems
             (which enlarge the space I
              move in)

             For your gifts
              (so instantaneous and like you)

For the striving and suffering and laughter
(I can follow you through
and share.)

For Ed

If you live
I shall rejoice

With us all.
If you die

I shall look forward
To my dying that much more.

Word Search

This search for words
Is a new hunt.

I treasure its pursuit
Of exactness,

As I trace lines
For myself

From myself
On paper

Stalking the sense
Within the event.

V

WOLF EYES
(1974)

FAIRY SHRIMP

A fairy shrimp
Has insides

So beautiful
It would dazzle

Anyone.

Haeckel—your
Watercolors, jellyfish,

Are as magni-
ficent as any

Living.

. . .

Nudibranchs are
Living images.

Mantis shrimp—
Your bubble

Was an egg sac.

Sea cucumber—
I pause

At your cunning.

Skate—your tenacity
Outlived

My hunger.

. . .

The ocean is
My fairyland,

The tidepools
My meditation.

Crab—beneath
Your ledge—

Enjoy the tides' new
Offering—your breakfast.

Old human coprolite—
You do not float,

Or dream enough
Of floating.

Two Poems

Over the edge
  Over the edge
    Up the ledge.

I consolidate
Incorporate structure
Build fidelity.

Everything is here—
Except the dance.

———————

Patiently I
Await madness.

Its release
A joy beyond joy.

Hunting Wildflowers

We slip
Up cliffs.

Flowers hang there
Waiting.

We examine,
Wonder as we slide.

In the high field
Each new discovery

Like a sudden Easter egg
We call out to one another.

"Wild radish, vetch,
Lupine, Johnny-jump-ups."

(California poppies
Peeking out.)

"Nudibranchs" I cry
In disbelief—

A tiny elfin urchin
Otherworld delight.

In real life
There is:

Owl's clover
Bear's claw

Sour clover
Blue-eyed grass

Soap-plant
Wild radish

And unknown
Star microscopics.

Night Walk
for Elizabeth Deutsch

A fairyland of pink puddles
                    and moonlight
A young girl's questions
                    about rape
Werewolves in the forest, creeps
                    on the streets.

We share our courage
Out on a walk, after dark
At the top of the world
High, intimate, careless, and enchanted.

Gogol
for Barbara Deutsch

Freedom to write
A story
Any way.

Make a
Nose
Disappear—

Forget
The
End—

Catch the
Fierce
Absurdity.

4:00 A.M.
for Leta Davis

Up late
I join Colette
And my dear remembered aunt

In an
Acceptance
Of this new hour

Its uses
My age
This new wisdom.

U.N. Environmental Conference

The Brazilian Delegate (his jungles the
   lungs of the world)
Shouts, threatened,
"There are *no* non-renewable resources.
   The Mato Grosso impedes progress."

The Vietnamese Delegate,
Oiled hair, perfect French,
Stands outlined against a background
Of burnt, bombed, poisoned forests

And speaks eloquently for a
  minor language change for
   an even more minor
    amendment for
     a most minor
      uselessly
       abstract
        resolution.

Tassajara

The jays—by the half dozen—
Eat figs and grapes, barely ripe,
Just a mite greener
Than you or I prefer.
Or . . . they wait busily
For bees to drown in the pool.

In the meantime, in between time,
It is hard work
Being beautiful,
Making all that racket.

Sound Poem

Clet—loud upon his shoulder.
Pflut—soft, felt upon my back.
Wind throws leaves from trees
At us, the porch, the ground.

They rustle now across the boards,
While cliffs *shuzzle* down
Small bits of dirt, dust, and twigs
Toward low still water now at rest.

The pool reflects back light,
Vibrates with shimmer of surface motion.
Different depths, inactive activity—
A pointillist painting quietly gone mad.

Ocotillo

Mesa Verde
Was red.

"Table top"
My mother said.

Young mind
Wrapped itself

Around the concept
Watching

Straight flat
Red mud road.

"Clay"
She said.

The mind did
Another turn.

. . .

My uncle's house
Appeared, alone

Stark center of
The mesa.

The wind howled
Making

Palisade bagpipes
A desert horn

Of his
Ocotillo fence.

SEA RANCH

Mind hunts white ceanothus
Out of season.
Reason knows no logic.

Desire for white surprise
Respects no time of year,
Heeds only the intricate inner ear.

IMPRESSIONS — TASSAJARA

1.

Ugliness arises,
Sinks back,
Like some strange figure from the pool—
A lumpen shape that never breaks the surface film.

2.

Flies crawl about my lips,
That search for notes
They cannot reach,
Parched, cut by rabbit's claw.

3.

Courage, gained from praise,
From him from whom I prize it most,
Wells up from toe to gut to head to hand
To fashion yet more images of strange new hue.

A Chinese Painting

The stairs,
Up the mountain,
Are delicately, barely visible.

A chicken looks at
A butterfly looking at . . .

                    I think of Issa.

Traces

Rollicking
Down dusty curves

The play is in
The gamble.

The love in
Life persisting.

THIRTY-NINE

Today I put up three new mirrors
Wrote a poem
Phoned an old friend.

I look Victorian
In the oblong mirror.
There's a vacancy
Where the fireplace belongs.

Round—beautiful
Light yellow grapefruit.
My lace nightgown.
The sound of our rat
            making a home.

Tonight Jane reads me
Emily Dickinson.
A new dimension—
She grows to womanhood
And faintly understands
            the love poems.

Her black mascaraed eyelashes
On her round pale rosy cheeks.
Blond snowy hair falling

Softly on round shoulders—
A bright life-child,
Child surrounded by her
            own beauty.

The house is rich
With flowers and mirrors.

My afternoon anger
Fades with Scotch
Accomplishments and beauty.

The flowers are gold,
White, yellow,
Rust red.

The mirror, framed by maple,
Brings the leaves
In
                    from outside.

OVERFLOW

The music
    the floors—
        his endless
            hammering
                ever leaping
                    ever sharpening
                    (help me!)
                    wit.

Harpsichord music
    shakes me.

He looks up at me
　　with soft brown eyes,

"We are
　　trapped in elfland
　　　　lovingly, together."
Fires burn
My wits reel
The intensity
Is quiet
　　and immense.

The Day after Forty
for Peggi Oakley

Is just like any other day
Except the treasurer got drunk
And voted everyone raises,

He went shopping with me,
And I sit in my new canopy bed,
And look into future years from under
　　　　　　wolfskin and velvet.

7-21-61

I dreamed I was an elf queen sleeping
In the forest in a wide orange nectarine
Contour belt—curled and uncurling.

To a Mattress, Velvet, and Wolfskin

Beautiful bed—
I lay there.

Rumpled wolfskin,
I shed you.

You rested
You comforted me

And your folds
Are dark brown

Filled with the love
My form and yours assumed.

My sensuality
My body

Your contours
Your life force

Together we
Entwined

Created this
Forever pattern.

GUESTS

1.

We have
Two newts.

Tonight
They ate brine shrimp,

Shed their own skins,
And ate *them*.

2.

Our rat
Died.

He was old.
He died slowly.

It was hard
For him, for us.

POEM

Flee   fly   flow.
Oh, oh, oh—

The price too great.
I meditate,
Instead.

MOTORCYCLES

Cycle, circle, cycle.
Around and back—

Why not, cut
Loose—

Cycle
Out?

POISED THERE
for Billy Gray

Balance, Billy, balance!
On a rope, on a surfboard, on a corner
On your bike at fifty miles per hour.

Hang there, spin on a toe,
Execute your dance, your play,
With level mind and steady body.

Sit, spin out thoughts deliberately
With that same steady balance.
Or slowly light with pleasure,

Raise one eyebrow in amusement.
Your fine nose, high cheekbones, and
Level honest gaze delight—my mind,

Bring close an image of my
Father, ambidextrous, making his
Backhand shots with ease, lefthanded.

WOLF POEM I

The wolf had amber eyes
That stared out
The back of a station wagon.

They caught me
Unaware—
Waiting, as I was, on the lawn.

My breath stopped short,
A little.
My heart freed itself.

. . .

A woman was
Destroyed by
Wolf love.

. . .

I give thanks
For my
Narrow escape.

Wolf Poem II

Wolves,
Yes, lean.

Wolves,
Yes, powerful.

This wolf—
Venerable also.

But without
Your eyes

Your eyes
Your amber eyes

I would be
Where I was
               yesterday.

MARIGOLDS

This morning, like wilted celery,
You hung from your vase—
Dismayed, dead, limp, and accusing.
I blamed the florist, but
Struggled still, unable to face
The signal of your demise.
Snipped, leaves stripped,

Fresh water, more space, and
Back to the table.
Tonight, rewarded, I watch . . .
Five faces, bright round and upright
Stare pertly from out
               fresh
                  stiff
                     green
                        leaves.

Outside Tucson

The sound
Imprints itself,

Becomes
The web

Of my soul—
Coyote

They call
It.

Not enough
To describe

        the event.

March 31, 1971

Large mysterious
Marble ashtray,

You were here
Before.

Before puberty rites
(not enacted)

Before individuation
(just now begun)

Before structure
(newly acquired).

You were here
When life was

Full, vigorous
Upward bound

Full of mixed
Beauty and pain

And mystic
Complexities.

Full of
Growing children

Full of power
Desire and ambition.

Pound says:
    Pull down thy vanity . . .
    Pull down thy vanity . . .
    Pull down thy vanity.
His voice quavers.
Power, pain, knowledge, and age entwine.

Tears burst upward—out.
    The time is here . . .
        The time is here . . .
            The time is here.

FETISH PIECE

Hedgehogs scratch,
Hedgehogs hedge . . .
I want to show the children

A fairy footed
Shy creature

Padding on quick feet—
Quick brow hedge
(I can feel the gesture)

The connection is
Inexplicable, complete.

Spines, abandoned,
Beautiful brown—light-black.
A garland or a fetish piece?

A Valentine for Mike

Because your eyes cross when you're eating
Because you showed me Old English
Because you brought me Monteverdi,
                    and Brahms.
Because you have the eyes of our child,
Because I burnt my sweat shirt and wear
Italian princess dresses now.

Because you need me and are beautiful.

Posited

Juxta posed:
Coffee—brandy.

The self deman
ding balance,

Hoping for . . .
Clarity.

Smell of
Roasted corn

Roasted coff
ee and fish

A puritan
Ex perience.

Roasting,
Tortillas toasted,

Root about
Nose first

Seeking pri
mary experience.

Words, Sa pir
Do form ex per ience.

The forest um
brella has

Tangled mirrors—
Art nou veau roots.

You can see
Through them.

THIRTIETH BIRTHDAY—HAIKU

The sound of the fire.
The orange flowers on long stems.
Why did I put the rugs down?

Searching

Care, care, care
Fully.

Step, step, step
Lightly.

Feel, feel, feel
Succinctly.

Lead, lead, lead
Cautiously.

Be, be, be
Rooted.

Root, root, root
For your being.

Nose the turf.
Paw holes.

Root, root, out
New truth.

ODE

I love owls
I love Jane
Full of howls
Running in the rain

Flying in the air
Wind in her hair
Perching on a stone
Harrying a bone

Flying thru the nite
Freer than a kite
Hat on a-kilter
Looking thru her filter

High cheekbones
Oval feathered heart
Eyes huge cones
Eyes that dart

Owl so free
Daughter so smart
Owl sits apart
Daughter *will* see

Loves of mine
That nurture me—
Be just a sign
Of all that's free and fine.

FREEWHEELIN'
for Frank Reynolds

How describe
Your clear madness

Your chauvinistic chivalry
Your instant compassion

Your hard insistence
On *knowing*—(as if he or we *knew*!)

Your pride
Or human godlike wrath

Your rebellion
Or your respect?

. . .

Yourself has etched itself
Upon us

. . .

Spirit doffing hat to Spirit.

A Vacancy

An old unconsummated
Love . . . hangs sadly
In my thoughts.

When passion is gone,
The moment—unspent—
Stands silent, accusing,

An abortion, neither buried
Nor born—its space
A vacancy.

Homer I

Reading Homer
High . . . thrilled:
A cowboy movie.

Real heroes—sweeping
Images—carry me
From page to page

Rapt
Throwing my voice
Into the tumult.

HOMER II

Reading Homer
Nameless Fear
Holds my heels.

I wait it out.
Finally, I shall tire
Or move.

A slight edge
On fear, after fifteen
Years of struggle.

HOLLYWOOD
for Michael, Stanley, and Tom

He sees frantic
        parasites on the dying body
                of a city.

I sleep
        in unreal sets
        and groan physically
                at unreal blood
                        and violence.

I tiptoe through
     perversion
     violence,
Hit jealousy head on,
     and blush at my
     stupidity,

Avoid the desk clerk
and feel rich
Surrounded by

Three men from Mars.

THE PHONE CALL

Mt. Saint Elias—
Rising sharply 18,000 feet

From the coast
Of Alaska—

I met there
Tonight

With my
Brother.

We spoke
For the

First time,
Not from passion,

Not from embarrassment,
But, directly from

Our mutual
Spirit.

It was quiet.
It was

Like meeting the wolf.

VI

EXTENDED LOVE POEM
(1978)

Fog lies still
In a long thin strip
Over the ocean . . . early evening.

A clear black
Sky above
Means . . .

The air is hot.
Outside, car noises,
Voices, begin to rise up, crystallized.

> *The outside is coming in.*

HEEDLESS

Camel sweater
Camel cashmere shawl

The real me emerges
From a cocoon of curly hair

Stands there sleek
And elegant—colors mine—

Haircut svelte
Stance freed of old fetters—

Life glows sure again
Against desert colors.

Color me brown
And tan.

Give me desert space
To stride in, hide in, and
                    bloom in—
A white cactus
Flower among thorns.

Thunderstorms echo
        pain and triumph.

PLAY

He misses the play
In me.

He plays.
I hardly notice.

Who will
Dance with me?

Bird twitches—
Afraid, but

Wanting action.
May I?

MY IMP

The Imp—my imp
The hidden delicious
Subterranean imp—

Conqueror of fears—
Master of the
Delicate lash—

Raises his troll head
Hangs his nose over
The wall

And laughs. Laughs
Hunting for sport
At anyone's inconvenience.

My full power lies
There with him
           and rises
Exuberant at its rebirth.

MEMENTO

A round welt.
A vein hit,
By what?

By a gesture
Made in anger
Sometime, someplace.

The morning after,

The wound a
Precise interesting hurt.
A mystery.

A reminder of rabid hissing hate
           which
Then passed,
Leaving an odd clear
Outline to reality

The way the desert
Looks—after a summer
Storm passes.

No rancor, only
Industry and clear sight
                which
Leave sharp outlines
Surrounding yesterday's
        rage.

AFTER FORTY YEARS

Three dented fenders
Three escaped rapes

Not a large tolerance
For damaging

        or being damaged.

EULOGY

My spirit drags
At your approach.

I cannot remember
For fear to say goodbye.

I cannot remember
For your dismembering

Blocks my path.
Steel doors clang down
At thoughts of loss.

Lost, I reach out,
Catch you in my heart's surrender

Look for you under a hat
Find you in a gesture

Love you in soft leather boots
Or in another man's singularity
        and wit,
                or
Stretched taut
Walk the streets,

A predator, afraid
To find what I desire.

Boy Haircut

Trim female
Hips

Above
Soft boots.

The mirror
Reflects

The parts.
The parts

Reflect the
Whole:

My life
My perfection

My high
Stepping pride,

Exuberance,
And an uncanny
 ability
  to sob.

FORTY-SIX

My day alone
A step into space

A place to
Slowly encompass

My sadness
Pace myself to

Yesterday's formality
Loving the clarity

Of language, the
Rain, the gray

Ocean, the clouds,
Filling senses

According to their vast
Need for space

Silence, clarity . . .

Time out

   Time away.

More Blessed to Give

You
Gave
Me
        the clap.

What
Shall
I
        give you?

Another
Man's
Ba
            by?

Or a
Hand
Full
            of crabs?

COMPELLING EYES

Avoid them, avoid them.
Save cremation till later.

And yet desire
The compulsion to be had.

Who do I love?
Who do I love?

Large brown eyes?
A steady fastidious desire?

A playboy?
My father?

Or the "other"
That forever "other"

Who refuses to lie
Between the lines

Thus existing nowhere
But forever there

A taunt—a step ahead.
My lure
        to where?

EXTENDED LOVE POEM

I   Love
      (that sickness, desire, and longing
      I hide from)
        Brings a blush under my cheekbone,
         A block to words
           A new fullness to my lips,
             Largeness to my eyes, softness
               To my ways, and a sudden startle
               (if I see you).
             My chest tightens,
           I am happy,
         Excited,
        Expectant. My
      Thighs tingle and
    I blush, smile quietly, and phantasize

Phantasies of
  reading you poetry,
    feeling your hands on my head,
      touching you.

    . . .

Comforting you
  care seeps out
    tenderness follows, burgeoning,
      and suddenly desire, full blown, is there.

    . . .

    The dam bursts.
     Tears of relief pour out.
Held back tenderness
Tears through me.

    Quiet tears join
     Immense tenderness, and
Flood through me
Toward you.

    . . .

I will hold you
  be there during
    your private anguish
      quietly waiting for
        your return.

I hold you, hold your being
  quietly in
    my two palms, carefully
      I hold you.

Later you hold me.
  Your hands frame my face.
    We enter a private world together.
      I abandon my being for now,
        your tenderness the scaffolding
          for my surrender
            for the first and still last
              proffering of self and spirit.

            . . .

My breasts warm
  reach out toward your touch
    assured of your care, desire, precise deep
    adoration.

            . . .

I come
  without wishing, knowing, or expecting
    such a thing—giving my gift
      unexpectedly
        to you, safely,
          before I leave.

The trust you build
keeps me riveted there
as fear catches me
and I wait afraid
until you lure out
my desire to overcome
my fear.

The trust I give you feels eternal.
I am sheltered by your steady lasting care.
I cry to remember, feel frail and helpless,
Happy that your ever thereness holds me so.

Pigeons fly away
Fly slowly back
As we savor these
Last moments, our lasting care,
and then say goodbye again.

II   Or rush to be held,
and find it gone.
A quiet sadness
or a raging NO

To burn
To exorcise
To punish
To destroy
To frighten with deadly enmity.

So—should I not rage—
to see gone he
whom I love more than all

He who has
    nourished me
    played with me
    filled each niche of my mind
        of my possible expectations
            of my absolute desire,
    who has rocked the universe
        with me in his arms
    has created ever new paradise for the two of us
    encased, encapsulated, tuned so finely
        to each other, each animal,
            each leaf, each nest,
            that reality stepped
                back two steps,
                left us the
                    original
                    Adam
                    &
                    Eve
    frolicking unashamed in Edens
    that changed place and time but never
        lost their innocence or total bliss
        or instant electrical charge.
        A laugh, a bite, a caress
            were all the same in paradise.
        We nestled there secure.
        A moment stretched, lasted, satisfied.

Your legs guided us, prevailed,
    and gladly was I ruled by your desire—
    depended on it—only able to follow—
        delighted "only" to follow and feel
            that charge of your entering and re-entering.

My dependency itself a release from myself.
My giving, opening new parts of me—
   as sudden as the loosening in my
     lower spine after peyote tea.
So often high together
   on nothing but each other,
     deer, and
        dreadful intimacy.

Your loss left such space
   that the dried leaf of my being
   hung on the frail stem of haiku,
solacing itself with words, as that winter
     of suffering marched slowly onward.
Anna Akhmatova said "God healed my
     soul with the icy calm of love's absence."
And so I waited.

III   Now I study love,
        Court it slowly
        Circle it, observe my fear,
        Love's ways, and daintily

        Dip in a toe
        For a moment.

        I write "I love you"
        Then rush to erase the feeling.
        But end in tears of acceptance.

        Why the tears?
        Why the tears?
        Why the tears?

Each time I circle
  they catch me
    my mind goes blank
      I sense the joy and step away.

Because it's true
Because I have loved you
Because I dare not now
Because I wish to try
Because I do love you
      but am ravished
        staked
        a butterfly twisting on a pin
          held here
          held here
          held suspended here.

          It is the suspense
          I cannot bear.

The suspense is a
          cliff waiting for me to let go.

The suspense is a dark cave
          I may fall into.

The suspense is suspense . . .
          forever hoping for the impossible
          loving the hopeless.

So now hung there, I continue
          snipping suspense
          and cutting love's thread.

The resolution I desire—an acceptance
       of suspense, of love
      as it occurs
          coupled with new
          control of the letting go.

IV   Lose my heart to a rabbit?
Fall in love with a chicken?
Love a black girl at first glance?
Be pierced by an intense boy look?

Bring myself to love instead of
Love surprising me?
What courage I
Will then possess.

     . . .

Or the smell of
Someone cooking for me
Caring for me

The smell of rain on creosote bushes
The smell of a hot horse
The smell of skin heated by the sun
Putting my nose in a clean dog's fur.

     . . .

The way I first saw
And loved him
Red hair, dark brown eyes
Through the car window—
A door and thirty years
Separate us.

. . .

You stood there
Unexpectedly, an old love's features
Accosting me from new
Quarters
     with that same intensity.

. . .

I saw you across a
Room full of heads. She
Said your name. Not
     again I hoped / feared.

. . .

We fell in love
There in the middle of strangers
Shyly intimate and pleased. Glad
     two days later we had not.

. . .

I lay my head carelessly
In your lap, and you
Possessed me warmly for
            the moment.

            . . .

Enchanted, ravished, breathless
I searched your face as your
Hand came into mine.
            "Take off my rings" I whispered.

            . . .

I leaned over the bar
Your warm eyes engulfed me
I basked, and could not accept
            your closure.

            . . .

Lips suddenly kissing deep deep deep—
Startling some unknown want
That strives to right itself, return from
            that spiraling desire.

            . . .

Across the dinner table
I listen politely, but study
The sensuality of your being
            as you study mine.

            . . .

Tuned to love's possibilities
I play and fill the botanical gardens
With sensual warmths, intimacies, lesbian
      undertones and endless sensual possibilities.

V   I see our perfect
Tenderness,
Feel the flow of all
I desire—
     and
Then your fat
Lecherous presence
Menaces my delicate
Sensibilities
     and

I come to lose
An unhealthy desire
For perfect endings,
And laugh a deep
     laugh of
Liberation.

For now.

For Amini

To press a rabbit close
To lose myself in a hound's eyes
Lie close to a horse's neck
Surrender to a falcon's
                    dark stare
            or
Long for a wolf gaze
  A whale's slow turning
    A dolphin's glancing sensuality
      An owl's soft fierce eye.

To follow a wave's curl
Mold my body to a hot smooth rock
Arc to a far horizon
Be one with a tree branch
      or a dusty desert mesa
            stomach down.

These connections are
        but longings
            for the "other"
Love for what skin can touch
            what the soul can desire.

NIGHT

Quiet gas hiss.
Leaves against
Wet windows.

The quiet
Holds my hand,
Reaches out

To solace
My soul
With leaves.

This chink
Of night
Holds me,

As I hold
Suffering
And turn

To look on
Peace, silence—
Growing things.

VII
HARD EDGE
(1987)

Hard Edge

The crow watches.
I wait upon anger
Now gone,

Wait upon it for
The edge only it
Gives,

For the clarity of
A cold eye,
After

Leaning
Too far
Out!

Collage

Quiet the tension
Pauses of interwoven silence
Smells, textures, buds
Tastes, textures, touches
Braid in with surprises.

. . .

Each new discovery as
Slow and quiet as a
Possum's front feet.

Pearls for Kathie

My pearls
Sit in the cupboard

And I feel sad
Seeing the opalescent

Colored contoured
Nacreous gloss—

Reflecting your
Cosmic eye

Which suffers
Sans hope

While I sit
Comforted

    by oak arms.

Still Life

Ranunculus
Make still lives
On my kitchen table

As delightful as
Van Gogh's shoes—

Hiss

A cat's reminder.
There are lines not to be
Crossed.

Is it a species that
Cannot
Interbreed?

I first wanted a
Falcon.
Longed

Dreadfully for him.
Met him in his eyes.
Held him as he died.

I still forget.
Desire a moment's
Crossover.

Need reminding.

JAMES

You caught my heart
And all you did was blink.

One half hour old,
With a look

That took away my
Breath—captured my mind.

    Big blue blinking eyes
    A large squeezed head
    Lined forehead
    A real bridged nose
    Two brow furrows
    A rosebud mouth
    Stout cheeks
    A skinny wrinkled neck

    And ultimate poise.

NIGHT

Wandering from room to room
Smiling.
How can life be so full at fifty-two?

For Kathie

If the world needs
Seven men

To sit in a circle
And suffer

For the world—
Can we not

Take turns
As well?

For Bob

Your wings
Sit on a bronze
Angel

Next to our
Cruciform door and
Our window

To the sea—
And your embrace

Lies in bronze
On our oak table

Emanating sensuality
Captured forever

In a space you
Created . . . that captured silence.

GARDENS

Opium, hats,
Flowers bending to a breeze

The patterns of sunshine
The taste of wine and feta

Avocados, limbs, shadows
The protection of pines

    The promise of pools.

SPRING '84

This year Spring came in
January. Untimely.
Uncomely.
       Not enough rain.

Nonetheless children roll about—
Fruit trees blossom.
Birds, everywhere, noisy.

Our calendar suddenly
Out of date; I study
Celtic Spring, Chinese New Year, &

Groundhog Day
Hunting for a broader base
For this unsteady "nature."

Even my year-old grandson
Waves hopefully at a
four-year-old blond
Strapped into her car seat.

SAPPHO

The spirit matters
Most of the words gone

The simplicity
And ardor

Reach out and
Catch a resonance

That time and fragments
Only enhance.

June 18, 1984

Bills, bills, bills
Thrills, thrills, thrills
Skills, skills, skills

metacognition
memory
&
metamorphosis

. . .

cocoon me out
right now!

James

He lies there
Center of the universe

Composed, yet curious.
What Gods graced you so?

TANKMATES

The killer whale
Carries the dead porpoise
    Tenderly

In his mouth
For hours
    While

Attendants try
This way and that
    To extricate

The dead beloved
From the mouth
    Of his companion

Who keeps still
His friend close to him
    Until
Time / loosens his grip
And mankind and sense

    Take over,
    Loosen his grip

        On loss
        On love.

VIII
TIME LOOSENS HIS GRIP
(1980s)

Conclusion

Lips, eyes, and hands
Hold our mind—

Shape the folds
Of brain cells

As we take in
And give out

Sounds, smells, skin sensations—
Shape ourselves by

What we see, what we touch,
By skin, by those other

Forms, shapes, visions
Which mold our mind

As our mind trains
Our fingers

As our mind listens to lips
Shaping sounds

As our mind tastes new thoughts
Feels new temperatures,

Focuses on all those
New edges,

And learns to look
Into those special eyes

Way, way inside into
The soul of those eyes.

For Robert Duncan

What holds us?
Lifts us?

Rings, clarion
Like, from beak

To heart—
Raising totality

To new-felt
Completeness?

Hammer to metal
Lightning to humid air.

Mind to idea.
Heart to image.

His voice
To my bones.

It happened.

THE LEFT-HANDED GUN

Thumb to mouth
I aim my desire
Where tooth and tongue
Extract the power

And reach
With what's left,
My right,
To shape the world.

COUNTRY
for Emily

We traverse ten acres
I love the difficulty of slopes.

We float down slow
Rivers.

Eat naked on the
Banks.

Wherefrom this unexpected
Pleasure?

Buckshee of age
And courage.

Robert D. on Mission Street

It's Mexico.
Voices from the street

Mix behind the
Poetry

Make it sound warm.
With music

Rising—faintly
As voices rise and fall

And poetry continues
Enclosed concentrated

Enhanced . . . by what
Falls away . . .

"The Systems Demand Their Own Use"
—*Piaget*

To vault *between* the horns
To escape between the teeth

Swallowed whole
To re-emerge

Intact

. . .

The challenge
Persistently demands
Action.

The action
Demands
Courage, nimble

Swift deftness.
"Rebirth" its own

Temporary
Triumph.

WOMAN

To be female is to sit at
the center of the
universe.
Women create it. It flows through us.
We are the first image,
We are imprinted
For a lifetime.

Our sensitivity makes us nervous
　　　Makes us empathize
Makes us good for young children.
　　Should we give this up
　　　　to
　　　Join them—
　Those who cannot
　　Control life?
　Those who need
　　Other power.

Caverns

I love
The caverns of poetry

Serve in the days
Of developing creatures

Work in the light
Of continuing reality

Delighting in the
Ambiguities of creativity

The divergences in
Growth

The sources, the nuances
The daily human ingenuity.

For Grappelli

The pause matters.
Intervals are essence.
The wait delights.

The breath's end
Brings pause,
A moment of eternity

An interval, a delight
The weaving of suspense
With one precisely timed note.

The Future Stops Here

My ears buzz with silence
Dreams of missed meetings
Torment my nights

The future stops here.
Doom hangs over
My hope.

God is not just.
Is He?
Is there He?

              Courage matters.

NOGUCHI

Your past opens
    My eyes.
I look again
    Now,
Make room for
    One more
        Lamp,
            The only lamp—
                The final lamp?
Your aesthetic fits us
    We admire your exquisite sensibility
    The vast scope of what you are—

And long for more   m o r e   m o r e.
    I want Noguchis for all
        Six compartments of my life!

            Your grace is
            Easy
            Dynamic.
                        Elusive
                        Concrete
                        Sensual
                        Sparse
                        Balanced
                        Etched
                        Considered

ESKIMOS

I reread your lives, over and over,
Swell with pride at your constant courage

Weep at the bravery in your tough dogged resistance

To circumstance as it closes in in the form of
    ice, blizzards, starvation, government
    ineptness intruding over and over and over—
    mindlessly and inhumanly sweeping your
    problems back under the rug time and time again
As the truth of the horror of mismanagement
    grows, as the dead bodies stretch out
    across the arctic, starved and diseased or
    struggle toward the last defeat—
    dole, where children have nothing
    to imitate and parents nothing to teach.
The inexorable hand of whom? Documented, there
    are many: The Canadian Royal Mounties
                     The Hudson Bay Company
                     The missionaries
                     The Indian officials
                     The government employees
But not one, not one man, you can face
    and struggle with—not one place you can
    force to acknowledge the problem.
But this is not why I trace you: I trace you to feel
and cry for your strength, your persistence, your honesty,
your simplicity, your fidelity to family, place, and human
values.   I salute you Owliktuk
                   Iktoluka

COASTLINE

You line my life
With red-tails on wires

Sparrow hawks "holding"
Sheep posed on hills

Wooden fences and
Brown-green fields.

Water stretched out, out, out and
To the north and south—
          Pale green, deep blue, muddy brown ocean:

Background which
Swallows my soul

As you change color
Season, sky, and beaches

But never lose your
Wildness.

AVALOKITEŚVARA

You sit   by the
Tall Kleenex box

Together you both
Comfort me.

A statue
An altar

And two mangoes
Complete God's

Care . . .
Centered in these

Five objects He shows
Himself through

plus

the five mice I
intend to trap

June Rains

Out of season smell
Freshens my spirit

In the midst of sorrow
    Sorrow which sneaked slowly in
        Without notice until the sudden hurt
            And holding back of tears began to tell

To tell me something more was happening
    To tell me it wasn't the words but the loss

That hurt—the happy glorious triumphant
　　Loss, in which you become mother
　　　Not just daughter, in which you
　　　　　Become your desire and struggle,

In which you become HIS, owned and
　　Owning a new future of complex
　　　Pain and pleasure, gamble, loss, love
　　　　Ties, tugs, turnovers, trials, revisions
　　　　　And endless rewrites . . .

MORAL ENDINGS: GOODBYE

Two hundred poems later, I find
And you don't mind

That those last two lines
Weren't quite right—

A mite too heavy
Perhaps too sterile

A peril to poetry—they
Hung there, abstract,

Self-conscious,
A summation no one
　　　　　Wanted.

FOR EMILY

I love roses, larkspur
Yellow jasmine, cosmos,

And staghorn ferns. I need
The taste of strawberries

Ripened on my roof
of dwarf figs
of ripe tomatoes
of maybe even peaches

  . . .

Emily has
 secret redwoods
  on stony acres
   where boulders are
    like bouquets for my eyes
and streams make a presence—
 make clay, make noise,
  make baths as we wander
   across roads we oil
    with crankcase waste
    and measure with
    string and
     compass

Present Danger

Like elk brought down
By wolves with
127 different parasites

Or Walt Whitman's
Autopsy when he died of old age
With many diseased organs noted.

. . .

Careful—the wolves
May spot me, single me
Out from the herd.

    My optimistic movements
      May confuse them.

Pax

White rose—so delicate, so fine
You sum up all the best of me.

Your delicacy, your sensitive unfolding,
Your sudden beauty, your many-stemmed blossoms

Giving all, lovely as they spend themselves
And come again all new and quietly vibrant.

Please

Water the strawberries
Leave the check
Send in the attendance
Lock up the saws
Say goodbye to children leaving
Leave a last newsletter
    But . . . don't pack
    Don't take the next step
    Wait
    Take a Stéphane Grappelli pause
    Find me in all this mess
    Stay with me for a beat

Engage Me—Enrage Me

You do that to me—still.
I admire your talent,

Despair at my cooperation,
For I am soooo adroit at sidestep.

Your ingenuity fas-
Cinates me in a morbid way.

Sometimes you used to make me laugh
With your grotesque physical funny games
And I was grateful.

Now you only move me to anger.
Still . . . it's a talent. A need.
Now.

I laugh with Patti

I love James

I wait, await our next tangle—
                    It's how we meet nowadays.

LSD

I am the wave breaking
I am the pause between breath

It rolls me relentlessly—
That ocean soul
Turns me on the wheel of time,
Cracks me open with relief

As it releases me
Spreads me on the beach
Slowly to sink
To be regathered and

Once more be drawn, tightened,
Brought to a peak and
Sent, or let go,
Released, racing down the crest—

Over and over and over and over
Until the wheel of life becomes a rack
Of pain, and I beg to be let off
To pass on to anywhere else where it isn't happening.

. . .

Now it is only the pause between breath
The stillness filled with the treasure
Of letting go, of non-being, the eternal quiet
Of life, of my body, of time—

A waiting where nothing happens
A stillness on the mesa top
A sunset from the rooftop of my adolescence
A moment caught while floating, or

Lying, looking up, from the bottom of the pool.
The smell and the space of the barn that day out of time.
A vacancy in which to find myself.
A timeless spirit exploring itself.

HEAVY METAL

Rage against a bad knee
Rage against your not knowing
Me.

Rage against a past
I barely existed in—in spite of
Central position.

Rage against drunken
Macho men you admired—
For what?

Wonder about
AIDS—
And think about your new
Morality—

Hardly a step in my direction—
Just a new precaution in an ever more
Dangerous world.

PERMISSION

You left me to re-attach myself
Carefully and only partly to someone else

While you finished your fling
With fast cars, married women, cocaine,
      magic, and deception.

Now you begin a new life
With a young strong lady

To whom you give fidelity,
Honesty, and clean living.

        Thanks.

REGAINED

I talk too much
Burn the vegetables
Hide things from myself

Living alone
There is no one
Here to blame

HUMILIATED

Hot tears—
Years flash past.

Who am I—
Not me, but he.

Apart I
Look back

Track my / his
failure

My / whosoever's
helplessness

With the hard
sadness of

One who loved
Us both.

PANDORA

And still at the end, at the last,
There remained "hope."

Its wings having carried me so far
Still are not too weary.

And I am grateful
For their support.

ROBERT AND JESS

Returned again—there at the beginning
I turn to you at the long slow end

Not understanding the connection
But pleased to renew the bond

Return a bit of the favor and
Replenish myself with your selves—
    minds, tastes, and sympathies.

Beginning to Say Goodbye

I study the shapes of new windows
Sort furniture, lean on the comfort
Of known objects in my life

Look sadly at corners created
With love, one by one,
Over the past quarter century

Flown so quickly and passionately—
Leaving these fond traces
In each special space

I say goodbye and plan
Braiding the two together
As I gather myself

With fear and hope for
The next step

December

Yesterday the Japanese anemone bloomed.
It had waited four weeks for
Last night's light winter rain.

And still this morning it showed
Its kiwi green center
Surrounded by yellow.

Its delicacy hangs in the air
Still.

Missing You

Left in rage.
A day apart.

Chewing the hurt,
The anger.

A second day of
Distress—plotting

Defensive retaliation.
The third day

Came mental bargaining
"I'll quit—you quit!"

The fourth day was
Sad regret—

Would this were us
Here, now, like this.

Wish you could love me
As you *can* love,

Know how to love,
But cannot do with me.

Wish, hope we might
Somewhere at the end—

Find a wild passionate
Place to meet.

Finally, it's called:
"Missing you."

STONES
for Steve Ajay

The ultimate love story
Unfolds itself slowly

Poem by poem
Image by image

Honed and refined
Spaced properly among

Familiar images
Chosen to lend

Reality and a certain
Suspense to a
　　　　Suspenseful reality.

Night Watch

Now there's a new "she"
Young, smart, caring.

And the hurt
Cramps my chest

Chokes my throat
Or leaves me

Sitting beside you
Jerking uncontrollably

Not even cold—
Just looking at the new you

The two new yous,
Twitching at "distant plans"

Aching, jerking, talking
Courteously and slowly

Trying to understand enough—
Afraid of each new answer

A trial of nerves
Lasting the night.

IX

THE COREOPSIS ARE BRIGHT AGAIN
(1980s)

June

New earrings reach
   my shoulders
      and swing.

The tomatoes grow large
   on my one green
      tomato plant.

They grow red on
   the plant with
      the brown leaves.

The coreopsis are
   bright again.
One flowered—blown on its side
      by the wind.

For My Mother

Grasp the moment—
"Don't ever forget me," he said,
His name now lost.

Where does it lie?
Deep in the bones
Of our spirit

A mysterious genetic
      Blessing!

Sensuality
for Betty

Black Russian cigarettes
  Pasta with clam sauce
    Elegant black jump suit
      Mozart concertos
     Firelight

       And your
           Blazing black eyes!

Alone

It seems hard . . . here.
Yet I choose to be alone.

It was easier thirty-five years ago.

Michael

You write poems now
    about Berkeley
    about peyote skies
And it doesn't matter that much
    for I know
    in another six months

She will exist
        only on paper
        in your mind.

BOWER BIRD

Sweet violin strings
Carry my swooning heart

Heart that swoons
With longing

Heart that allows
Brief longing

Playing with
Sweet anguish

Walking the line
Of loss

Hoping for
Sweet passionate reunion

        Afraid my bower bird
        Has lured a new female.

Riding the Waves of Me

Bumpy—a sea full
    of whitecaps.
The waves break too soon

But there's always one more
    to catch—
An idea, a rug, an animal,
    a boulder, or a new love.

Will I ever ride lightly
    on a calm warm sea . . .
Or shall I stamp out snakes
    Worry a dead bird
        Struggle up steep slopes
            Looking always for the
            Next ideal spot.

    No Zen for me.
    This time.

Helix

The cross of my life
Lies in the
    pain
    pleasure
        helix
In my desire
    and
    fear

In my stability
    and
    wildness
In my stonewalling sexual passion
    In my total abandonment.

    Today I sat with it
    For awhile.

FOR LAWRENCE

Overcome with your good looks
And my new freedom

I study old photos
Listen to high-school swing bands

And wonder . . .

    Jay with one lung gone
    Gorgeous academic paintings
    Sell for big money

    Shirley—delicately and
    Quietly sensitive and wry.
    I love both you and our history.

And love YOU, L., your Rémy Martin eyes
With dark lashes keep me fixated

On your profile wondering anew
At your personal beauty

That I have studied so long
And from so many angles

And still find it rivets me
Leaving me empty when I pull away
All the better to see you again.

AFFAIR

Michael—You and
Simone could

Never have had
"The love affair

Of the century."
We had already

Had it
Together

And you
Didn't even

Let me know
You knew.

Sighting

That luminous golden space ship
Lifted from between soft purple hills

Miraculously and slowly
Shaped itself into a full moon—

Orange and then later
A white orb, Japanese,
    Between pine branches.

Remembrances Accounted For

Alone in our tent
The Pacific below us
A meadow circled with pines on three sides
Awakened at dawn by strange strong thuds
    I look out . . . a herd of horses
    Beautiful in the early morning mist—emerge.

Later—camped in a forest
    Thick with leaves where no one walks
We emerge in the early morning.
Lie on our backs and watch ospreys
    Circle overhead, fish dangling, screaming, or searching.

In Baja we paddle immersed
In sky, water birds, and landscape
Noiselessly cutting the water with
    Our synchronized paddles.

At Ventana we watch white kites
See a daytime great horned owl
    fly from an oak tree from our horses.

In Puerto Vallarta we
    Celebrate thunderstorms
    And look out shuttered windows
    Onto a quiet warm lagoon, pigs frolicking.
    We shower in outdoor tropical elegance
    Read Neruda out loud.

On mules we ride to
    Snow-lined lakes
    Swim—hunt wildflowers
    High with the altitude and the search
    Descend to ride up again
    To camp among boulders and
    Watch the sunset over
    A wide Alpine meadow.

ME, HERE, STILL

Short hair
Stubby to the touch

Reunites me
With me

The past recedes
The "I" remains

Some weeks
The center

Is strong.

BABY BIRD

You loved me—
As I waded out

Returning the
Baby bird

To its mother—
Waiting beyond

The breaking waves.

And it was seldom
You let it surface.

We both were careful

. . .

Wading out
Chest high

Past low
Breaking waves

She returned
The beached

Baby bird
To its mother

And he loved
Her sudden gesture.

And her being.

1989

As the jasmine
Gathers strength
    to climb the fence

As the blue hibiscus
Blossoms, and blossoms again—
    a startling color—

And Japanese anemone
Wait—a deep green, promising
    leaf rosette,

The yellow rose to come
Sends out yet another long, deep
         green-leafed branch.

The redwood tree
Thickens and shelters the stacked
    cut pine from the park.

A native ceanothus stands tall while
The spider plants spread below
    the cut-back fuchsia.

Old ivy holds up the
Fence where honeysuckle
    makes its way.

Clover and blue campanulas
Edge the lawn near the
    newly planted magnolia.

Calla lilies and berry bushes
Sneak in under the
      less-loved cypress,

And an orange cat watches
Unnamed finches and
      large lovely doves

While the black cat
Tears noisy pieces of rush
                  from my doormat.

The cold dry clear December skies
Finally cloud, brighten lights below

And let go a soft
Welcome drizzle of
      much-needed rain.

DEDICATION

I dedicate me to:
                  Truth
                  Beauty
                  Irreverence
                  Eroticism
                  Romanticism
                  Reality
                        And all growing things.

Committed irrevocably to:
        drab colors
        taste, touch, movement, and smell
        daily occurrences
        the past
         and
            those loved objects:
                a mynah bird
                a Chou bronze
                a turquoise bracelet
            people:
                husbands
                lovers
                children
                families.

THE OCEAN

My real draw
Always there

Beyond reach
Shimmering promises

Mysteries, depths
Unachievable—sirens—
                shoals.

CATHARSIS

3:00 a.m.—the mind
Reaches—into senex,
Into puer—into
The exterior as the interior—

While my body
Struggles to purge
Itself of old grief
Or new rigidities

With help from a
Myriad of chemicals.
(Should I, instead,
meditate?)

The search explores,
Reaches toward
Africa, India,
The depths of Denmark.

Fierce rebellion
Wild animal freedom
Tender human connections
Fine sensibilities

And the ability
To be lost and found
In dreams with
Their own landscapes,
       Their own life.

These all leave me,
Leaving, for now,
Everything to the
Living past—

As a tribute
A salute to . . .
The bonds,
The shared ideas, ideals.

Money, property,
Never seemed important,
But we made it
Between us.

What I seek now
Is my imagination,
My dreams,
My other world . . .

IMAGES

I trust the thrust of each image,
And am not led astray,
But carried through sensually
To a completeness of visual pleasure—

Intimate with new green growing knowledge.

. . .

I trust each thrust.
I trust the thrust of the thigh
The thrust of each tightly rounded muscled shoulder
Which leads to

The thrust of the neck
Pulsing and strong
Leading to the thrust of the head
The thrust of the brow and high cheekbones.

Below the softness of the wild full curved lips
Mix with the infinite grace of a curved wrist
Which leads down to a hand in repose
Its strength and ease might be Blake's God caught in
                        the act of creation.

But I look up and your eyes are there for me
And I trust myself to their depth
And hang there satisfied,
To never look away.

Haiku

Obsessed with shining
The moon isn't even full
Was the rabbit fed?

Memory

A small oblong bedroom
Nine feet by seven feet.

A horizontal window
Placed—high up.

Two feet by
Four feet.

A large round moon
Hung in desert air outside.

I watch from under warm covers
Am filled with still silence.

Somewhere . . . from far away . . . out there . . .
I hear . . . the long howls calling . . .

        stillness   still.

Winter Light

after the film by Lawrence Jordan

Races on and sweeps me up again
Thrusts me into the sky,
At the top of tall branches,
Leaves me hanging mid-flight
        suspended in air.

Brings me down, lifts me up,
Sprays me on the beach
Lets me float in quiet pools reflecting
All the shapes growing on my banks

Or I trickle slowly down a craggy rock
Making my way over and over again through
Deep dark mysterious cracks
Until I see sheep etched there on the hill

And early morning light fills the sky
Behind real branches making real patterns
That make my heart dance with excitement,
While that light, that quiet dark early light

Fills my soul.
I can feel it expand.

DAWN REDWOOD

Barbara would know your botanical name.
I sit here, stare at your every branch and growth,

See your ancestors
Rediscovered a thousand years later.

See you standing a hundred feet tall
Sun shining through your needles, brook at your feet.

They say you are deciduous.
I wait in disbelief.

You, with unconcern,
Sprout yet new, lighter green leaf-tips.

TRUST

I find myself impaled
Suddenly, unexpectedly.

A white lie
Lies exposed

And I blush with betrayal
Stammer, lose my way—

And gradually recover.

It's my marriage
Repeated again

Through this charming
Woman friend who

Betrays as thoughtlessly
Heedlessly and casually

As he did.

DARK BROWN
for Jean, Jeanine, and Monica

Those sunflowers with
Giant black-brown centers
Salomes with brown and yellow
                Dappled leaves.

   . . .

The dark brown
Of Baudelaire
Verlaine and Mallarmé.

   . . .

May we never lose
Both sides of the coin
The depth—the terror.

   . . .

The delicacy and
The laughter
The music and the words.

KWANNON
for Kathie Bunnell

A rose for the leaf space
Held up by that deep blue vase.

My eyes trace the veins
That form the patterned web

That stands on ostrich legs
Whose necks bend to beauty,

Lead to the mountain that
Holds the vase that cradles

My mind—here—suspended in time.

X

Our Love Overleapt the Chasms
(1990s)

IRREVERENT

Please God let me remain
Until the end
    Irreverent.

Please God grant me
A slice of mischief
    Big enough
To last this lifetime.

I WANT A POEM

I want a poem
As hard as a gold nugget

I want a poem
As clean and clear
    as an Eskimo life.

I want a poem
As fine as
    Musk ox fur.

    . . .

I want to capture
Our spirit
    and
Find a wall
To hurl it against.

Now
for Michael

The empty field
Made way

For the dream.
The dream

Was a feeling—
A feeling I feel
now.

A full feeling
Inside, between
my legs.

I lie here.
The dream makes
way

For remembering—
For remembering
the feel

The feel of your
Cock—Your full
cock

Pressing inside me.
My arms stretch
wide

Across the bed.
My heart opens with
gratitude.

Grateful for that
Full first opening
to you.

Later it changed
And I never told you.

Now I know.
I tell you now.

GREECE

Crooked toes.
Crooked streets.

I pray for
                Transcendence
                Direction

                · · ·

In the middle of
All these gods

Surely one
Is listening.

DEAR NANCY

You would have loved
This ambience—

The glitter,
The sophistication,

The reflections
On the water.

I miss what
We were—
       Searching,
       Breaking through
       With wild laughter

       Seeking truth
       Seeking outrage

          Hunting for a place—
          Together—to transform—

             Each—our own—anger.

             I still search.

                Wish you

                   Were here—

                     Joanna

My Man

My man has
Thick rosebud lips.

When fringed with beard
His sensual nose,

Inviting lips
And high cheekbones

And strong jaws
Would not fail
    To catch my
        Attention.

My Sixtieth

These cusps—awkward.
Almost aged
    but

Still clinging
    To the past
        To youth?

My dreams of aging
    Explode—gradually,
Mirror the slow
    Disenchantment
        With marriage.

These underbellies
    Always catch me
        Finally.

        . . .

Still a faint hope:
Over this horizon,
This uphill trek—

Perhaps a lovely
Downhill slope?
A pleasant meadow?—
An end to rocky
            Sojourns?
I have learned
        to pray.

1990

From the still hot tub
We listen to wisteria pods
                    exploding.

Jupiter bright in the East
Orion rising through pine branches.

We inch sensually toward
A new year, a new decade.

A haiku feast
And buttery wine as

The afternoon's lovemaking
Recedes and out "there"

Governments turn over
Like exploding pods.

LAUGHTER

I sense that "universe of laughter."
It lies out there—remembered from

Marijuana highs in my thirties
It hangs out there somewhere—

James writes on psychology and laughter
I remember "Laughter and the Pancreas"

How Thich Nhat Hanh says a smile
Relaxes x number of muscles in the face

How Indians in India meet
Each morning—to laugh together for fifteen minutes.

How I led a class of older adults
Laughing together—all I had to do was begin.

How I miss and cherish laughter
How I must not use it to laugh at others.

But how they, and I, are funny.
How Jane makes me laugh till I pee

How I savor the marijuana I save
Waiting for it to take me to laughter

All those surprises—the funny surprises
Bruce or Kevin or Herb Caen brought me—

Life's treasures.

ROCK

The hollow sound—
Rock hitting rock.

Down the hillside
A man works

Stacking random rocks—
"Just cleaning
up," he says.

But a pattern,
"a maze" he calls it,

Emerges. "I left
A seat—that flat rock there."

No heap—this job
The pleasure of creating.

AGING

I pray more
I forgive more
I expect less

Yet, it's not
            Peaceful.

THIS LOOSENING

The need to "do"
Drops away.

I lie in the hammock
Feel the gentle swing

Watch the changing light
Through the arbor's rose leaves.

At night dreams are
Busy—very busy

But the days relax
Expand, and the year's work

Slows to a stop—
Looks back.

HAWKS

Golden sweeps of light.
Lying on my back I

Swirl in your now
Van Gogh sky

Overwhelmed with
Mounting excitement

As I catch you
Suddenly again close-up

And the gold flashes
And disappears

And flashes again
Catching light—

Lifting my soul
To float and dive

With each of you
As you crisscross

My sky
Fill my eyes.

My back against
Hard dry brown hills.

Let Out

4:00 in the afternoon—
The clerk says

"Duty finished"

Out of here!

Let me kick
The dust of Justice

From my feet!

Old Poems

I look at your depth,
Texture, valleys,
Crevices, peaks—

And wonder at the
Even playing field
Of new poems—

As level in their
Gratitude and quiet
Pleasure, as were

Those early endless
Descriptions—descriptions
That propelled me away

That led me into new
Searches—into an Extended
Love Poem.

DEAR ALBERT

You struggle still
Argue with her death
    Miss all of us

And tonight I,
Here in Greece,

Have time to
Miss our misbegotten

    Early struggles.

I remember you
        Lying in the gutter of a Mexican
        Border town—drunk—without money—laughing
            as they came to roll you.

I remember you
        The story of you tied to a pickup
        Running behind drunk, laughing, crying.

I remember you
        Dancing the dance
        Of the seven veils
            With an erection.

I remember you
        Exploding bombs
        In your swimming pool
               Behind gravestones.

I remember you
        Pulling Billy's
        Limp body out.

I remember you
        Telling your mother
        There was breath on the mirror.

I remember
        Dancing, stripping for you,
        Drunk in Guaymas—
               in our hotel in Guaymas.

I remember
        Hearing the Yaquis
        Coming to kill us
        On the island in Guaymas.

I remember
        You sleeping at the foot
        Of our bordello bed to keep
               The "Toad"—the drunken
               merchant marine "Toad"—
               at bay.

I remember
        Collecting clams in Guaymas Bay
        With the local Indians—
               Where the sewer emptied.

I remember

        Cooking us horsemeat and
        Serving it by candlelight.

I remember

        You reading army survival manuals
        Perched in the tree outside
            While I cooked and
            You grew hungry.

I remember

        Collecting prickly pear
        On our honeymoon
            (it cooks up sticky).

I remember

        The diesels that couldn't help
        When we ran out of gas
            On our honeymoon.

I remember

        The preacher who wondered
        "Why we needed to marry so soon"
            And I wasn't even pregnant.

I remember

        When your high school love said
        "No more" and my heart went
            out to you.

I remember

        When she phoned and talked and talked
        And I ran away jealous to the mountains
            And you slept unworried.

I remember

>When you went to San Francisco
And I rented our house
And came too.

I remember

>Our hotel, the street of strippers,
The first late night homosexual
>>Bar where young good-looking
Men in Brooks Brothers suits sang to
Each other in a crowded bar over a piano—
>>>And I was the only woman.

I am sixty and look at

>Old Greek women in black
Look at their wrinkles—at
>>my future.

You are many wives and

>Children away from me,
But I need to remember
>and tell you.

I remember

>You threw the knife.
It hit the wall of our river house
>butt first, and went in.

I remember

>The goats in our yard—
Losing my virginity in that house.

I remember
> You playing the guitar,
> Barefoot, feet on the table.

> Company due, the house a mess—
> And I in wrath piled those pictures

> That bikini you loved, in a pyre
> And lit them all as you watched laughing
>> nervous and horrified.

I remember
> Your mother's wisdom,
> Her softness and intimacy and humor

> Her tender courage—I was so
> Young when she chose me

> Took me aside
> To tell me it was Billy's birthday
>> How old he would have been
>> What he was like.

It takes thousands of miles
And many years for all this
> To make its way
> To paper—but it has been with me—always.

Nearing Sixty-Two

A quiet calm descends
I drive through tall trees—
A piano concerto
                accompanies me—

The notes—clear—present.
There is time sitting parked
                to hear the end.

It is like descending
The stairs at Shell Beach,
                time is suspended.

These moments of grace
Settle upon me—enter me and
                I am grateful.

            . . .

In the park, dark
Sets in slowly as
                mosquitoes gather—

And children are carried home
Tired, dirty, satisfied
        a few at a time

And my being soaks in
The richness of their complex
        lives

A bare maypole in my hand—
The next to last to leave.

A Long Moment

for James

The playground quietly occupied.
Street traffic constant and quiet.

Bicycles and runners on the sidewalk.
And there—in that expanse of green grass,

Silently, a great blue heron stands.
Its calm centered poise rivets

Our attention. Indeed, it is
Hunting. Not fish, not here.

We watch, absorbed in the
Absolute centered quiet stalking:

The arched neck coils.
It strikes—nothing.

Still we watch. That concentration,
That motionless movement

In the middle of quiet dailiness
Absorbs us. The older boy

Joins the hunt, constructing
Nooses from shoelaces,

Waiting patiently by holes.
The heron strikes.

A small furry object
Hangs from its beak—

Disappears, and we watch,
The boy watches—the two

Hunt. The boy's movements
Meld with the heron's.

The sky is marked with clouds.
The sun is fading—is not present.

The green hillside holds the two.
The boy—the heron

Move with grace,
With intention.

The heron—five times—
Succeeds.

The boy watches each gopher
Make its way down the heron's throat.

Contained, we watch.

To Wander Mad

To wander mad the streets of my mind
To rub out my eyes—finish with sight
To pull out my hair—tear at the roots
Of all this being called *me*
To finish with reason—to scream out
With pain—to trail my mind in
The dirty gutters of despair—humming

Cockles and mussels, alive, alive, oh!

Eben

Eben—I call to you.
Every evening at dusk
My heart whispers your name.
Longing as strong and deep as the tide

Pulls me toward—
What can never be—
But what once was—
A love that did not die

When death came.
A love that remembers,
Sighs—and once—last night—
Broke silence

Wailed a mourner's cry—
Cried your name over
And over—gave my heart
Full space to cry out for you

Felt the anguish, the loss
And hurtled my soul into the unknown
In search of what cannot be.
Oh, Eben, Eben, Eben—I cry out to you.

YOUR PICTURE
for Almyr

There is a picture—you with
Our mother, I pause—look—see

Your face—your hand's
Tenderness—on Mother's arm,

And tears spring out.
Tears for the years of care

You've given me, her.
Tears for the naked sensitivity

And pain you carry with you.
It's there in you at six

In another picture—already
The stalwart older brother—

Hurt by what? But full of courage—
A knight and poet at six years old.

                    . . .

Later you sing to me
Read me Keats
Share ideas with me
Watch over me
            and
I bask in your approval
Admire your mind, your ideas.

                    . . .

Later still—seeing you, each time,
I cry because you make my heart so full.
And between times, forever, I know you
Are there for me—without seeing
                        hearing or
                        talking to you.

                    . . .

And now we share our mother's old age
Coming together out of a mutual spirit
We sip spirits—compare stories
Wonder at our love of sex, love of risk,
    . . . Or you puzzle at our differences.

And I am proud, proud of your
    Imagination, your intelligence, your will,
    Your stubborn anarchistic spirit.
How rich I am that you keep
        dreaming
        scheming
        caring
It pleases me to share genes with
         such as you!

LISTENING

To the waves
On the freeway,

Lost in myself
I see a girl—seventeen—

She stands in
A green wool dress

On a rock above the ocean.
It's summer—she's in love.

He stands behind her
With his arms around her.

A wave breaks high
And they are wet, laughing.

I remember her clean clear heart
Her open trust—her round confident body

And I cry tears
To see such young pure loveliness.

INTERLUDE

Cat in the garden
Moonlight and crickets

Not the pause between breaths
Not cosmic bliss

Not tranquil death
Or the forgiveness I pursue

But a moment of mine
Out of time.

Facing West

The low mountains
Form a dusky background

For the lower mountain's
Softly jagged outlines

Against sky
Against the "other."

The church spires
Catch pink light.

The birch tree
Bare and white

Against the Norfolk Pine.
Inside—white shutters.

Outside a crow calls.
The sun takes so long
           To sink.

Facing West 2

The sun is sinking.
I take a warrior's stance.

This dusk
I face head on

With an acceptance
An acceptance of sinking

Of the pain of surrender.
My immense desire,

Unresolved, may become
A pearl I wear inside,

To crack open from
Time to time.

. . .

This dusk
This ebenglau

My keening
Remains silent
It is part of my joy.

WALKING

Yesterday—my feet
Caressed the earth.

With each step
They caressed the earth.

Pleasure ran up
My legs.

The sky was bigger,
The earth rounder.

The sidewalk
Was psychedelic.

. . .

And I—I was
Part of it—
In a new quiet
Thrilling way.

Buddhist monk,
Has it always all been here?

CASA MADRONE

for Lawrence

We look through these windows
Thirty years later

Blessed with the silky
Soft water of the bay

The open doors
The good food

The city's lights
The sailboat lights

And this night—
A grace of clouds

Of light
Of acceptance

Of new beginnings and
Friendships over coffee

Renewed—So rare now—
Space to spend time.

And again tonight
Time stretches.

As if high, we watch
A new generation

Expand, luxuriate, and
Delight us as we sip wine

Remember beaches and marijuana
And how children come alive

When we stop the busyness
For a moment—
                now and then.

        The sweetness of Grappelli's pauses.
        The delicious moments
        I strive to live in

                Eluding me mostly,
                By grace granted tonight.

TOBAGO

for Lawrence

The air is body temperature
The water is soft
The waves brush the quiet beach

The persistent bird sound—pshwee, pshwee
Starts at 4:00 a.m.
Raucous parrots pass through at 5:00

You lie here beside me
Sleeping lightly.
A quiet sadness lies within me.

Last night's hurt, familiar,
Travels with me through this balmy night.
My company here again in early morning light.

These last two postcards
Stamped and empty—
What, how, to say anything now.

CONNECTIONS

My reality
Lies in the voice
    of the red-tail hawk.

My reality
Lies in the bent grass
    where the deer lay.

My reality
Lies with
    the ripe blackberry
    with white clouds.

My reality lies
In the voices of my
    ancestors—

Teaching me place
Silence, touch, seeing—
    beyond sight.

Teaching me focus,
Connections with
    other worlds.

These—all these—gently
Brush my mind—stir
    deep spaces.

MOTHER NECESSITY

In the midst of joy
It's necessary to give

Pain its due,
As it is necessary

In time of pain
To reinvent beauty,
    Re-discover laughter.

DEAR BOB—
DEAR SUE—

    My special loves
    You came . . .

    My heart jumped.
How is it your hearts
Make mine so joyful!

Not just your care
But all you are to me
Made today an EVENT.

It is your compassion—Sue
Your courage and mind and future—Bob
But this is not it and this is not it
And this is not it—And we are not mystical
But what we each bring
One to another IS.

And words are not it. I sit with each of you
In a time beyond time—in a time I don't recognize.
In a time I challenge myself to describe and avoid—a
mystery I may not wish to describe—but one
for which I thank the force that pushes up the grass.

*[Party to celebrate my new face and Lawrence's spring garden,
May 1997]*

HAY TRUCKS

Fifteen years ago—you passed
Me—soaring along the highways.

Each time I wished
"Let me always love him."

Now you pass me by
And still I wish, each time

"Let me always love
Like this."

Once—having loved
So completely, so totally

There is no going back.
The person matters

Matters always and forever
But the "love" can never be gone.

Great God, bless, bless, bless you
For opening my heart so late in life.

A gift that time—death—a person
Can never take from me—from life.

The Ritual

Hemingway sharpening pencils
H. D. "One glass of wine a sacrament."
A slight longing for immersion.

Would the drop into imagination
Be like my plunge into cold Pacific waves? . . .
To be preceded by Irish whiskey . . .

Lured on *by* the phantasy—the phantasy
Of staying dry on a surfboard—
Drawn by the waves until

The cold water becomes an afterthought—
Each swell a new hope/challenge . . .
Until bitterly chilled I re-emerge once more.

Colette locked in her room each morning.
Virginia Woolf chained herself to the typewriter.
The work would not be entered easily.

Is this late night ritual a beginning?
And what would I be chasing?
How could I give up an instant,

An instant of all this reality?

A Prayer
for Joan Bullington

Can I bottle love
Market it

Give money away
Live in Mexico

Laugh, make parties
Make love, dance

Take in stray children
Love dogs, hug horses

Add on to houses
Swim in the ocean

And keep that love
Flowing endlessly?

Race cars, gamble
Have adventures
Learn Spanish
Practice Yoga

Build an empire of
Love and roses?

NIGHT CRAWLERS

This night belongs to the crawlers.
Sow bugs, babies and adults, climb
Slowly on all those legs
Up and down the softly lit shingles

Pincer bugs cross and re-cross
The plastic cover over the nearby machine.
Patiently they examine
Each hole and then move on.

Out there in the dark
Slow snails make their
Way up thick sunflower stalks
And patiently feed on large leaves.

. . .

Sappho's world was that
Simple—and airy—and true.
Her words hang there—
So apparent they arrest you.

. . .

Together and apart we heal
Our wounded spirits of yesterday,
Moving quietly among flower beds
Paint, cutouts, and simple food.

The day closes; angels fly through
Your head and I deliver flowers,
Have quiet conversations, wait for
Further instructions, further illumination.

Yellow and black tiger swallowtail butterflies
Flit and sip at light blue lilies of the Nile
While giant sunflowers on short stems
Wait outside for tomorrow's planting.

The cat catches a night moth.
A small dead mouse lies
On the square stone path.
There are fresh dirt piles—gophers.

There are fresh eggs
Gifts from the boy and chickens
Next door, the boy I
Explore the yard with,

The boy who does not see
But feels his way, probing
This new space with questions,
With his white cane, with

Touch and with his sense of smell.
As we go about together
He brings me his new reality—
Such a deep voice, such a different world.

I have loved two deaf
Young men—those intense
Searching eyes reached
Inside of me.

Now I search for words, a
New kind of connection—
Shy to introduce touch
With this new noble young friend.

ODE TO A MATTRESS

You are leaving.
Thirty years later
You are leaving.

Where will all
Those memories go?
What will happen

To all the sensual
Delights you received?
Surely they are

Bedded deep within
Your softened insides.
No way to frame

And keep your
Rich presence here.
Sprayed with concrete,

Exhibited, would your
Testimony to delight
Shine through to crowds of strangers?

Or should you be collaged
With pieces of photos—
Parts of faces and bodies—

Bodies of all the lovely ladies
All the gallant randy men
Who bedded there.

A cross above your
Headboard to honor
All that lust,

All that life that
Passed moaning,
Crying, laughing, bouncing

And rolling over your
Receptive soft
Surface.

Somewhere, somewhere
You are immortal—
In concrete, in my memory, or

In vapors trailing skyward.

CHRONICLE

How many times
How many places
How many ways

Have we coupled.
Let me name them:
First, shyly, in your hot tub.

Then, part of your film, I stroll
The garden. After, later, when
We come together naked—

"Marry me" you say
And I melt into your
Eyes, your arms, but

Answer honestly "Never."
Love you always, yes,
Marry you, though, never.

Each hay truck is
An excuse to wish
"May this love last forever."

We meet for an hour—
Here, there, wherever—
And it is instant, total

Surrender to your whole body
Your whole soul, until
I wrench myself away—

Return to reality, work,
Life, and the phone call
That arranges our next meeting.

In bars, on hillsides,
In your car, in a motel,
At your house, in your teahouse.

Lunch at golf clubs.
Baseball games at bars.
Borrowed bedrooms with that

New baby sleeping in the
Other room. Cigarette bars
Where he sleeps in his carryall.

We began where he began
In his mother's, my daughter's,
Belly—under a full moon.

You took another
To live with you.
I raged, but

We continued—a blanket
And poetry in the trunk

Of your car.

You tired and she left.
We met in that mirrored bedroom.
Reflected, I couldn't separate your legs from mine.

Shy in that room, I
Confessed an earlier, past love, and
Suffered that love until you drew out

My desire, and I could
Lay the past to rest, and come
Again, to our love, your arms.

And so it went on.
Tears of joy to see you
Above me.

Tears of separation
Each time I left.
Joy, each return to heaven.

Reading H. D. aloud in the teahouse
Until we coiled together, or
Naked on a rug on the lawn.

I smelled your skin
Hot from the sun and we
Entwined again.

Or read *Ancient Evenings*
Or *Form in Nature*
At an inn in Mendocino,

Or watched a full moon
Over the ocean by a
Statue of St. Francis,

Or discovered the sensual
Delight of wooden Russian architecture,
Landscaping, smells, and tastes

At the inn we still
Return to—showering
Outdoors among the redwoods.

I took endless pictures of
All those gorgeous flowers and
Flower arrangements—

Or of you—still photos for
A 16 mm film. We filled our
Love, our time with images

Now seldom viewed—
Testimony to that total
Adoration, felt and recorded.

And then gradually, quietly
Slipping into everyday

Being with one another.

First one or two days
Then three days,
Then four

And lately the intimacy
Of this broken leg
Bringing us together

For months now—a
New kind of intimacy
Unavailable otherwise—

Which I savor and
Enjoy in my new dependency,
Your steady care

And our new closeness—
Shedding tears as I leave
For ten days—knowing

You won't be with me,
Wanting your nearness,
Treasuring this enforced honeymoon.

Slowly my independence
Hovers in the month to come.
The harvest moon slowly rises

And I am happy and loath
To take these new steps
That lead me back to my

Separate life, away from
The daily togetherness with you
The delicious nearness of

Your new body,
Our long luxurious
Lovemaking.

My God, shall I never
Tire of leaving you
Only to return again?

I could write a long book
Of love poems for all our
Travels, all our fights,

For all our joys and sorrows
And dinners and pleasures
And friends and plans

And disappointments
And rages and returns
Endlessly spiraling about us,

Leading to the
Next poem.

To a Rose

There—in a three-inch pot—
You sit, one year later
And blossom.

Watered by rain
And occasional attention,
Your strong spirit

Sustains itself,
Delights me,
Yet once again.

The Gathering

The weeded grass has turned brown.

Stars shine outside.

Inside, my head reverberates
With Verlaine—good company,

And that piece of psychic grit, of sand:
"A nice little feminine heart"

Which will not be turned into a pearl!

Thunder

Storms rage.
Feet pace.

No illumination here.
The desire to

Split apart
For love

Makes vacancy
A slowly seething

Cauldron.

This Birthday

This birthday
Being alive

Is my present.

My Path

I study the "way"
See it beyond me,

Persevere as I sit,
Daily, find new prayers

And daily repeat
Old prayers

Struggle with
Interior "bad seeds"

Dedicate my way
Toward what I pray for:

Grace chips for me
Blessings for those I love.

Baja

I swam with a sea lion,
Her initials sprayed on
With peroxide are A H.

We moved together, danced.
This dream lived
Excites me, fills me.

. . .

The skies excite me
The clean motion of the kayak
Pleases my senses.

Black and white sea eagles
Stand on cardón cactus limbs.
Ospreys fly past.

A blue heron stands elegant
Against the cliff—on the edge
Of a huge stick nest.

These evening skies
These desert beaches
This life-filled water

These ash rock shapes
Those red jeweled crabs
That ring-tailed cat!

. . .

Every day my voyage
Seems complete.

WEE NIGHT CREATURES

Wee mealy bug, sow bug,
You cheer this late night.

The silent black cat
Sits nearby.

The fountain
Bubbles behind me.

A frog sends out
An occasional solo "rivet."

ENGRAVING

Like your engraving—I stand
Behind, to one side of,
The long open door.

Outside, night light
Makes a Palmer sky
From black clouds and a large moon.

I stand still . . .
A part of
That other picture

That engraving
Of a woman
Leaning in the doorway,

Her spirit
Quietly reaching
Out . . . into diffuse world light,

Which calls to her
As the moonlight
Now calls to me.

Thanks

Thanks to the Universe
For one more night
Of poems.

FIRELIGHT

Space to dream in.
You gave me a place

To place a dream in,
Hearing your voice—

A way to explore
That space, that place.

. . .

I tiptoe into your life.
Brave but afraid

Of reality
Of what I may find—

Or of a wall—
Or of no space—

Or no place for me
In all that I saw,

All that I felt,
All that fired me

Toward you by firelight
One January night.

. . .

The wonder of wanting
Freed my heart—

To adore,
To dare dream

An old dream
Once more.

Dreams

To dream of cyanide,
     The slow working,
          The wait for death,
               The desire for perhaps
                    One more experience.

     So slow, so real
The dreams of blindness—
          led from the seashore—
The sudden aloneness imposed
          and the fear and struggle to hold together.

One soaring dream—
     flight still demanding effort—
          only lifted from the ground—
               still navigating inside.

Where are the larger landscapes?
     The clear water streams, the
          Deep quiet ocean pools?

With drugs and drink I once
    danced—liberated—a newness.

Dreams of figures in a long hallway:
    Upset by my approach,
        The two statue figures
        Topple from the chair.

I saw them as silhouettes,
        One on the other's lap
          from behind,
            Then—
Tumbled, mannequins, ghosts.

She Writes

She writes
Usually alone
At night
  drinking

Now she writes
Seldom, drinks
Seldom, but
  tonight

She sits in the window
Sips and smokes
And waits,
  remembers

Her childhood roof
Alone at night
The city hers,
    still,

With stars and
Lights and un-thought,
Unfelt feelings, feelings
    waiting as

Thoughts waited
To be thought
And places waited
    to be found

Horses' heads
Chinese horses' heads
Etched in stone

Their jaws outlined
Nostrils flared
Ceramic heads

Foreign heads
Mythic heads
An image apart

The smooth flanks
The muscled chests
Their sleek legs

Ready to carry
Me—ready to
Feel my hand

On their backs
As skin ripples
And head turns

To search my
Meaning.

Moments out of time
Like the pause between breaths
Like the still air before
The rain when air turned rose color.

Knitting while the doctor
Performs his surgery.

Playing the flute
Outside the dying husband's door.

The stillness of death,
The eternity in a quiet infant

The smooth silken skin
Of a rising cock

A horse's soft silken
Nose.

Nasturtium leaves
Enchanted me then—

Before they had a name—
When they were a magic shape

Edges like pie crusts
Centers off center

And veins—oh those veins—
Still green as the leaves

Slowly aged and turned yellow—
As I watched my bouquets

In brown Mexican glass
Turn and transform.

Outside, climbing, reaching
Throwing out bright orange blossoms

Trailing the ground toward
Sunshine, re-seeding

Intertwining with rose.
And orchid leaves

Making tiny baby leaves
Or giant fairy leaves.

XI
LIKE AMOEBAS WE COOPERATE
(2000s)

This New Millennium

This gray cat
On this white Flokati rug—

This harp music
My grandson's plans

For a European tour.
Those ferrets

In their three-story
Condominium

Enrich my life
Beyond belief.

A New Note

Aah—and there is the ferret's sensuality.
Sliding noiselessly through thick white Flokati rugs

Rolling over, twisting, rubbing those long lithe
Beautifully relaxed brown and white bodies

Against all those different textures
As they look up appealing to your appreciation—

Their never-ending persistent curiosity
Leading them to ever new adventures—

Trying to enter, or to dislodge
That special object, fast feet working,

Or their total letting go, feet dangling,
Body soft, eyes beginning to close,

Or their trust, simplicity, warmth
And deep, deep, limp sleep,

Their love of each instant's happening.

THE SIMPLE

I study grief
But long for
    cigarettes and cognac

I meditate
And long for
    illumination

I listen to Mexican music
From across the lot
    and drink margaritas

I hear children and laughter
And look at
    the end of life

I swim in cold ocean water.
The desire to join with the "other"
                    remains

I am rich with past joinings
And poor only with what little I withheld
                    from others.

I gather sunflowers
I pick nasturtiums
        I love the simple

My love escapes into
The faint fragrance of roses
                    unpicked.

Exploring My Heart

At breakfast
        Tears come

Describing a remembered scene:
        My father's wheelchair—
        Near the goal posts—his bent form—

And off to the side, at a distance
        Unseen, I stand.
        My heart

Aches, but does not cry out
At all that love, at my helplessness.
       At all that love.

A GENERAL THEORY OF LOVE

As I fly toward poetry—
Suitcase filled with
Early love poems

And quietly look back,
Look back at those
Times,

At their record/poems
Left as trails, trails recorded
From an interior

An interior often lifted
From somewhere inside by
Solitude and cognac.

Where did it all go?
And how many missed
Being written

In the whirl of living;
Loving, searching, losing
Working and forgetting?

How easily the heart
Still leaps up toward
A loved face.

Even a remembered
Presence can bring tears
As the heart opens.

Your Future

James—I hold
You in my heart

Each day I hold the light for you.

Knowing: only
You and the universe

Are in charge
Of your future.

A Phil Whalen Specially Requested Evening Meal

7:30 p.m.—coffee with cream and sugar—medium strong please.
        apple pie with ice cream—if there is some.
9:00 p.m.—Roquefort cheese and crackers from in the cupboard.
        French olives—both kinds, please.
        glass of Merlot 199?.
9:30 p.m.—hash browns with sausage and catsup.

    . . .

Critiques: pie has too much cinnamon.
    not too much cheese on each cracker, please.
    Merlot a bit sour but okay.
    olives quite fine.
    hash browns and sausage—better than those burnt meatballs.

[Menu recorded at Zen Hospice sometime in 2001]

A White Cat

A white cat on a black roof
In the rosy pale dawn
Walks and leaps
Valentine's Day

SOMETIMES

Sometimes my soul cracks open.
It's the pause between breaths,
It's the space that time in the hammock creates,
It's Grappelli's wait for the next note,
It's the hours between life and death,
    The hours suspended away from duty,
    The first days of the furlough,
    It's the "One Endless Night of Love,"
        That space out of time
        That brings tears from the cracks
        Of a nowhere from somewhere inside.
        The crust of being parts—
Allows endless non-time to open the heart.

GRATITUDE

My gratitude
Remains constant

For my childhood
As it happened

For my passion
As an adult

For my rich past
As I age

And unabashedly—
For all my sensual pleasures

For my daughter
For my Ashbury Street

Home and creation
For those old and new ferrets

For this constant
Lover in my old age

For the home and garden
He created here

For his steadfastness
And integrity

For an occasional
Poem

For my friends
For knees that

Carry me down
And up stairs

For a neck that
Doesn't spasm

For a broken leg
That healed

For a new
Car I love

For an old
Car I wrecked

That didn't
Damage me

For former alcoholics
Who inform

And inspire me
For the length

Of this life
Span

For the losses
I have shared

And the depth
They bring me

For all those
Dead friends

Who remain
With me still

For my ancestors
I am created from

For this rich
Variegated universe

I am part of
For the purple

Weeping beech
That may never grow

For two magnolia
Which do grow

For my secret
Garden Lawrence gave me

For the redwood tree
I inherited

For the home I
Inherited

For Jess
Who is still here

For that
Daughter

Her husband
Her boys

My rabbit-ear fern
And all the art

In my home
Created by friends

I love and
Admire

For the graceful
Women in my life

For the irreverence
And humor

I have shared
And cherish

Free to well up
After the blackness,

Despair, and hopelessness
Faced earlier—

Looking at the
Shame of these times

Created by my
Country—this

"Advanced" technology—
With its lack of soul

Its lack of
Compassion as

It races toward
More goods

More prosperity
Less understanding

Less connection
Less heart.

LUST

I long to give this body—
Not to science, not to the fire.

I long to be given, whole
For the fish in the sea to nibble away.

I long to be buried, naked,
Under the earth, to be returned to the earth.

I want to be placed high,
On an altar made of sticks, for the birds,

For the birds of prey to feed on,
For the sun to whiten my bones.

I long, long to join myself
Back, back into all that life

From which I came.
I long, long to feed life directly.

THE MIND

The mind
Slips this way
   And that:

Hear the crow
Cawing—see the broken
   Limb—

My arms around a
Tree trunk—
   Resting.

Tree energy rises
Restores, protects
   Quietly

Someone tied a
Yellow green scarf here
   On this branch.

WRITINGS: BUCKSHEE

Pen to paper
Once more

Writings I
Call them

Sounds of crickets
Sounds of splashing fountain

Stillness
My breath inhaling

The sweet feel
Of cigarette to lip

This waiting—here—
Apart

Fern and shingles
At my elbow.

Where is the soul?
All about me.

And in this smoke
In these spirits.

AGAIN

We came through
Yet again.

Back then we waited
Apart—one hour

Until we found
One another.

Now we parted
And came together

In the same morning—
Parted this time

By our own interior
Desperate landscapes

But our love
Overleapt the chasms

Of psychic pain
And we were rewarded

As our wisdom has
Slowly grown—
　　　　Allowed us to come together.

FOURTH OF JULY
for Mary Turnbull

The first real holiday
Middle of the week

A remnant of special days
Not just a long weekend

Throngs line the highway
Above the beach

Bumper to bumper
Into Stinson

Then: our epitome
Of graciousness

Opens her home to
Family, friends, dogs

Who wander in and out
Chatting, walking, eating

Until the perfect day
The perfect ocean

The perfect people
The hot sand and dogs

Under their own umbrella
All meld together.

Only the fat-tired
Dune buggies

With helmeted police
To add an ominous note.

ODYSSEUS

Sin gets harder
        And harder.

No cigarettes
        In the freezer.

Hips hurt
        Navigating the window sill.

No matches and
        Chinese hand torch

Sticks and doesn't light!

                . . .

Yes, here I am   Not a moth cyst
78 years old   Not a silver fish
Celebrating   Not the vanquished *E. coli*
Mourning   Not the yeast cell destroyed
One more   But the coming death—
Lost life:

            Of my dear, warm, furry companion
          Who has, for five years, enriched my life
            With his bright expectant face
          Looking up at me—"what next?"
        His always hopeful question.

Yet always his acceptance
Of life as it is—

As, still, he quietly looks
For food he can't eat

Or licks his vitamin treats
From my finger
    With real pleasure.

Labors over to the sandbox,
Or turns under his towel,

Hunting for some comfort—
Possibly not a possible comfort.

Oh . . . I sigh . . . and don't yet
Light my cigarette—

Because it won't fill
The hole your leaving

Will leave in my life.

[For my ferret five weeks before he died]

THE ARGUMENT

We are all one
Like amoebas we cooperate
Create these structures called *aeropuertos*
Doorways to the air—and then,

. . .

Then we fill them with stores
Disposable fast-food courts
And clean restrooms, where we
Pass one another, without a bow, without a look.

DOWNSTAIRS

The caricatures come to life
   Mexicans, Asians, lively Blacks
Here I can relate
   Here my Buddhist desire for oneness
Comes alive
   Meanwhile all forms of humanity
Stream past—the number
   Confounding this desire to relate.

UPSTAIRS

Upstairs they have
    Blackened catfish and oysters
I want to connect with these hordes
    Of people, now thinned to
      Those a little richer.
And still they look like frozen mannequins
    So, unable to find souls, I
      Resort to Hieronymus Bosch.
Why not enjoy the absolute grotesqueness?

METAPHOR

The tsunami
Seen from a hillside video camera
Advances slowly, serenely
Carrying trucks, houses, trees, trash.

While in frame right
A distant car drives, heedless,
Down the highway toward
The tunnel to town.

My Poems: Chunks of My Life
for Glenn

Eviscerated, naked, vulnerable
And all I did was

Hand you three books
And a handful of more poems

"Like the sea cucumber," I said
That empties his insides

Into the waters of perceived danger
And swims away, empty but free.

[Pátzcuaro]

Vodka

Is drunkenness then
Truly a search for God?

I pick my way carefully
Because indeed I have gone elsewhere.

One inch beyond is
Sickness, despair, need.

Parceling out the day
    Until your German music
    Ensnares me, holds me here

Knitting needles joining threads as
    My heart soars and falls and catches
    To your horns and drum beats and violins

To want nothing more than to listen, to be
    Carried in and out and up and down
    As Mahler's Ninth rolls on carrying me

Back, back to being nineteen, a virgin dreaming of
    Lying in bed Sunday mornings—together
    Making love, souls entwined, listening to opera.

The sun has crossed the patio
    Lighting inside the candles which frame
    The large Mexican platter on display

And fruit trees out the back window move gently
    As the sun moves westward warming
    The sand-colored walls behind potted Yucca plants.

Big Sur and Mahler hang in memory together
    As here in Pátzcuaro black clouds
    Cover and then release a trapped sun.

I remember Jonathan's name.
    Michael's first book and his child
    Arrive the same day, to his wide naked brown eyes.

As Mahler's Ninth begins I feel the dance in it
    Knitting and moving to it, my mind
    Weaves memories, sitting in my brother's perfect couch.

The skies, trees, this feeling in my chest
    Must come as one nears dying
    The blessedness of it all being so present.

[Pátzcuaro]

Notes

Some of the poems in this volume were previously published, a few in slightly different form, in the following publications:

Chapbooks

McClure, Joanna. *Wolf Eyes*. San Francisco: Bearthm Press, 1974.
———. *Extended Love Poem*. Berkeley, CA: Arif Press, 1978.
———. *Hard Edge*. Minneapolis, MN: Coffee House Press, 1987.
———. *Catching Light*. San Francisco: Sore Dove Press, 2010.

Anthologies

Carlsson, Kristian, ed. *Kvinnas beat: 9 poeter från beatnikeran*. Malmö, Sweden: Smockadoll Förlag, 2009.

Charters, Ann, ed. *Beat Down to Your Soul: What Was the Beat Generation?* New York: Penguin, 2001.

Ciuraru, Carmela, ed. *Beat Poets*. New York: Alfred A. Knopf, 2002.

Knight, Arthur, and Kit Knight, eds. *The Unspeakable Visions of the Individual*. California, PA: Unspeakable Visions, 1980.

Knight, Brenda, ed. *Women of the Beat Generation: The Writers, Artists, and Muses at the Heart of a Revolution*. Boston, MA: Conari Press, 1996.

Peabody, Richard, ed. *A Different Beat: Writing by Women of the Beat Generation*. London: Serpent's Tail, 1997.

Peabody, Richard, and Lucinda Ebersole, eds. *Gargoyle: 20th Anniversary Edition*. Washington, DC: Paycock Press, 1997.

Rothenberg, Michael, and Suzi Winson, eds. *Continuous Flame: A Tribute to Philip Whalen*. New York: Fish Drum, 2005.

Journals and Magazines

Beatitude 31 (1981); 33 (1985)
Bombay Gin vol. 5, no. 1 (1997)
Café Review vol. 13 (2002)
Discourse 20, nos. 1 and 2 (1998)
Transit 22, Autumn (2009)

The Io Poetry Series

The Io Poetry Series honors the career work of poets who express the depth, breadth, and scope of subject matter of *Io* and North Atlantic Books. The Series pays tribute to North Atlantic Books' literary roots in *Io*, the interdisciplinary journal founded by Lindy Hough, Richard Grossinger, and colleagues in 1964. *Io*'s single-subject issues laid the groundwork for North Atlantic Books' literary publishing of subsequent decades. The poets in this series either appeared in the journal, were working concurrently, or preceded and inspired *Io*.

Westport Poems
Jonathan Towers

Heavenly Tree,
Northern Earth
Gerrit Lansing

The Intent On:
Collected Poems, 1962–2006
Kenneth Irby

Wild Horses, Wild Dreams:
New and Selected Poems,
1971–2010
Lindy Hough

Collected Poems
of Lenore Kandel
Lenore Kandel

Catching Light:
Collected Poems
of Joanna McClure
Joanna McClure

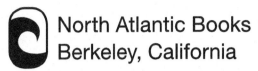
North Atlantic Books
Berkeley, California

Personal, spiritual, and planetary transformation

North Atlantic Books, a nonprofit publisher established in 1974, is dedicated to fostering community, education, and constructive dialogue. NABCommunities.com is a meeting place for an ever-growing membership of readers and authors to engage in the discussion of books and topics from North Atlantic's core publishing categories.

NAB Communities offer interactive social networks in these genres:

NOURISH: Raw Foods, Healthy Eating and Nutrition, All-Natural Recipes

WELLNESS: Holistic Health, Bodywork, Healing Therapies

WISDOM: New Consciousness, Spirituality, Self-Improvement

CULTURE: Literary Arts, Social Sciences, Lifestyle

BLUE SNAKE: Martial Arts History, Fighting Philosophy, Technique

Your free membership gives you access to:

Advance notice about new titles and exclusive giveaways

Podcasts, webinars, and events

Discussion forums

Polls, quizzes, and more!

Go to www.NABCommunities.com and join today.